W9-BNN-441

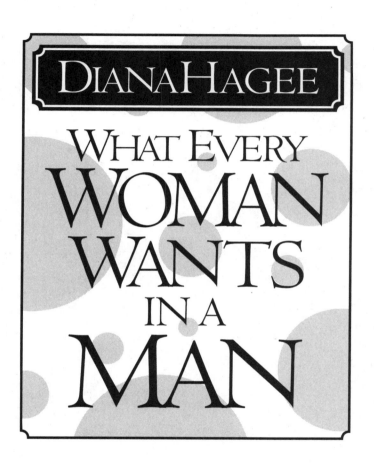

DianaHagee

What Every
Woman
Wants
In A
Man

Charisma
HOUSE
A Strang Company

Dedicated to the only man I ever wanted,
my beloved husband, John Hagee

Acknowledgments

I want to express my profound gratitude to:

- My King, who has taken me down paths I never thought possible

- My precious children, without whose loving contribution to our lives this book could not have been written. You are a treasure to me.

- Teresa Weaver, my dear friend who encourages me toward my divine destiny

- The members of Cornerstone Church, who have blessed our lives beyond measure

- Dr. Anne Reed, who willingly contributed her experience and hours of her time to this book

What women want in a man may not be what God wants them to have.
What women want in a man is not as easily received as we may think.
We have much to do with what we want from others.

—DIANA HAGEE

Diana Hagee is the chief of staff for John Hagee Ministries. John Hagee Ministries telecasts Pastor John Hagee's national radio and television ministry, which is carried in America on 160 full power TV stations and, 50 radio stations, 8 networks, and can be seen weekly in 99 million homes. John Hagee Ministries is in Canada on the Miracle Channel and CTS, and can be seen in Africa, Europe, Australia, New Zealand, and in most third world nations. She and her husband, John, have five children and three grandchildren.

CONTENTS

What Women Want
IN A MAN

> Therefore a man shall leave his father and mother
> and be joined to his wife, and they shall become
> one flesh.
>
> —GENESIS 2:24

> What God has joined together, let not man
> separate.
>
> —MATTHEW 19:6

YOU HAVE OFTEN heard it said that the most important decision you will ever make is whether or not you receive Jesus Christ as Savior. This decision will determine the quality of life you will lead on earth and the eternal life you will have in heaven.

The second most important decision you will make is whom you will marry. This choice will contribute to your future happiness and whether you will be able to serve the Lord to your maximum potential.

The God whom we serve created the world for our benefit. He created marriage for our benefit as well. You and your husband were created in the image of our Creator. He shows us through His infinite mercy and grace the steps we need to take to be all He ordains us to be. We are His children. Our marriages were planned by Him. He shows us what we must do to walk in harmony with our spouse to make our unions the beautiful blessing He has intended.

Most women I know are either looking for a husband, content with the one they have, or wishing they had a better one. When you ask men and women to give the reasons they married, you receive answers such as:

- We fell in love.
- We were physically attracted to each other.

1

- My friends were getting married, so I figured it was time to do the same.
- I needed stability and security in my life.
- Everybody expected us to get married.
- We "had to" get married.
- Our parents did not want us to marry, so we eloped.
- It seemed the right thing to do.

If we as Christians believe that God created marriage and has a purpose for it, then we must conclude that most of the reasons above are not the right reasons for marriage, nor can these reasons sustain a marriage. Christian marriage counselors Randall and Therese Cirner, in their book *10 Weeks to a Better Marriage,* sum up God's reasons for marriage this way:

1. To become one flesh
2. For committed love
3. For mutual service[1]

Rebbetzin Esther Jungreis, internationally acclaimed Orthodox Torah teacher and granddaughter, daughter, wife, and mother of rabbis, in her wonderful book *The Committed Life* states: "Our culture has taught us to equate love with gratification—with getting rather than with giving, with taking rather than sharing, with being our own persons rather than feeling a oneness with our mates. Therefore it's not surprising that people go in and out of relationships, since the returns are bound to fall short of their expectations."[2] In order to have successful relationships, we must stop living by the laws of this world and begin to live by the dictates of the inspired Word of God.

Whatever your marital status, you should be aware of the attack of the enemy on the traditional family in our society. From the beginning, the serpent attacked the covenant God the Father had with His people. Today is no different. When the church competes with the world in the divorce rate, *something is not right.* When the Word of God commissions the church to be in the world but not of the world, yet we mirror the world, *something is not right.*

Things are not right because we use the world and its standards as our life guidelines. We have failed to follow the guidelines set before us by the Potter who made us, the Savior who died for us, the Spirit who is there to guide us.

What are these *things?*

Scientists are being heralded because they devised a camera that shows a twelve-week-old baby in his mother's womb smile, walk, and yawn, yet our society demands stem cell research using the brain cells of these very babies. "Something is not right!"

There is an increase in sexually transmitted diseases because the "safe sex" purposed by the world is not! Fifteen million new cases are diagnosed each year with an annual cost for treatment of nearly $10 billion![3] When prescription drug usage is on the rise merely because our society would rather turn to a chemically induced euphoria than to lead a righteous lifestyle that produces an inward joy, "something is not right."

When the father is absent from the home and the child is looking for a leader in the gangs of the street . . . when the Supreme Court of the land rules that to regulate child pornography is an infringement on the freedom of speech . . . when we, as a people, must petition our government to issue a constitutional amendment that only recognizes a marriage between a man and a woman . . . "something is not right."

The divorce rate soars in America because our word is no longer our bond, and "covenant" is something we find in a homeowners association contract but not within our marriages. It is no wonder that women in our church come to me requesting prayer for their marriages, asking, "Please pray for my marriage . . . 'something is not right.'"

In the following pages of this book we will examine the relationships between the sexes. My prayer is that if you are a female reader, you will be able to glean what is necessary to choose a godly man, learn how to meet the needs of your husband, and benefit from a beautiful, long-lasting marriage.

If you are a male reader, I pray that you will learn how to attract a godly woman, learn more about giving a woman what she wants and needs, and learn to create a satisfying, lifelong marriage covenant.

I want this book to help you "make things right."

My husband, Pastor John Hagee, surveyed our congregation of several thousand people and asked the questions, "What do men want in a woman?" and "What do women want in a man?" Before I discuss the results of this survey showing these desires from a woman's point of view, allow me to share some research of my own.

WHAT I WANT IN A MAN
(WOMEN SURVEYED—AGE 25)

1. Handsome
2. Full of charisma
3. Financially successful
4. A caring listener
5. Great sense of humor
6. Physically fit
7. Fashionable dresser
8. Well mannered, appreciates the finer things
9. Full of thoughtful surprises
10. An imaginative, romantic lover

WHAT I WANT IN A MAN
(WOMEN SURVEYED—AGE 40)

1. Nice looking (hair is preferred on his head)
2. Opens car doors, holds chairs
3. Has enough money for a nice dinner
4. Listens more than he talks
5. Laughs at my jokes
6. Carries bags of groceries with ease
7. Owns at least one tie
8. Appreciates a good home-cooked meal
9. Remembers birthdays and anniversaries
10. Seeks romance at least once a week

WHAT I WANT IN A MAN
(WOMEN SURVEYED—AGE 55)

1. Not too ugly (bald head is acceptable)
2. Doesn't drive off until I am in the car
3. Works steady, splurges on dinner occasionally
4. Nods head when I am talking
5. Usually remembers punch lines of jokes
6. In good enough shape to play cards

7. Wears a T-shirt that covers his stomach
8. Wants more than nachos for our romantic night out on the town
9. Remembers to put the toilet seat down
10. Shaves most weekends

WHAT I WANT IN A MAN
(WOMEN SURVEYED—AGE 65)

1. Keeps hair in nose and ears trimmed
2. Doesn't belch or scratch in public
3. Doesn't borrow money too often
4. Doesn't nod off to sleep while I am venting
5. Doesn't retell the same joke too many times
6. Is in good enough shape to get off the couch on weekends
7. Usually wears matching socks and fresh underwear
8. Appreciates a good TV dinner
9. Remembers my name on occasion
10. Shaves some weekends

WHAT I WANT IN A MAN
(WOMEN SURVEYED—AGE 75)

1. Doesn't scare small children
2. Remembers where the bathroom is
3. Doesn't require much money for upkeep
4. Only snores lightly when asleep
5. Remembers why he is laughing
6. Is in good enough shape to stand up by himself
7. Usually wears some clothes
8. Likes soft foods
9. Remembers where he left his teeth
10. Remembers that it is the weekend

WHAT I WANT IN A MAN
(WOMEN SURVEYED—AGE 85)

1. Breathing
2. Doesn't miss the toilet[4]

This is obviously written to make you laugh, but sadly there is truth in the fact that the older the woman, the less she expects from her marriage. The graph I plotted from the responses we received to my husband's survey shows that the longer a woman is married, the less she expects positive changes to occur in her marriage.

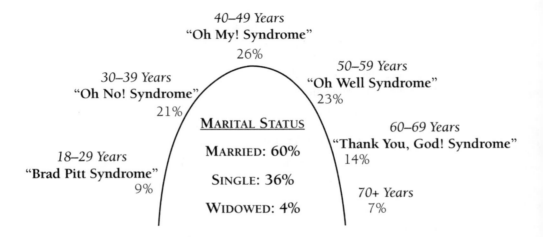

40–49 Years
"Oh My! Syndrome"
26%

50–59 Years
"Oh Well Syndrome"
23%

30–39 Years
"Oh No! Syndrome"
21%

<u>MARITAL STATUS</u>

MARRIED: **60%**

SINGLE: **36%**

WIDOWED: **4%**

60–69 Years
"Thank You, God! Syndrome"
14%

18–29 Years
"Brad Pitt Syndrome"
9%

70+ Years
7%

In the eighteen to twenty-nine age bracket, women have what I call the "Brad Pitt Syndrome." They are looking for beauty, passion, and illusion. Women thirty to thirty-nine years of age are wondering what they have gotten themselves into. I call this the "Oh No! Syndrome." Women ages forty to forty-nine are realizing what they feared at thirty has now come to pass. I call this the "Oh My! Syndrome." At ages fifty to fifty-nine, women resign themselves to the belief that their spouse will never change, or the "Oh Well Syndrome."

Finally, we have the age group of sixty and above. These women have learned to bring out the best in their spouses. They have learned that their word is their bond. They have learned to follow the voice of the Holy Spirit within their relationships. They realized that it is not their jobs to change their husbands. They have empowered themselves with the strength of God to defuse situations that were designed by the enemy to destroy their marriages. These women have surrendered to the Lord and allowed Him to lead them in wisdom and discernment. They are not victims; they are victorious! I call this the "Thank You, God! Syndrome."

Whatever age group you are in, I want this book to provide hope for you as only the Word of God can. I want you to be excited about what the Potter can do in your marriage. If the Lord can hold the heart of a king in the palm of His hand and turn the king's heart like rivers of water, then He can turn your marriage into something that resembles heaven on earth!

My section of this book should be entitled, "What Women Think They Want in a Man, and How to Get It!" My husband tells the story of a wealthy father who employed a nanny to care for his strong-willed child. As he sat in his study, he heard his son cry out. Immediately he called out to the nanny and asked what was wrong. The nanny calmly replied, "Oh, nothing, sir; your son is simply crying for something he wants that I am not willing to give him."

"I demand that you give my child what he wants!" the father commanded.

"Very well," replied the nanny.

Suddenly, another cry came from the son, much stronger and more intense than the first. Irritated, the father screamed from the study as he ran toward the nanny and his son. "What in heaven's name did he want?"

"A wasp," replied the nanny.

What women want in a man may not be what God wants them to have. What women want in a man is not as easily attained as we may think. We have much to do with what we want from others. This section will try to equip women to receive from others exactly what they need to receive in order to be the best women, wives, and mothers our Creator intended them to be.

The chapters of this book are based on the answers we gathered from my husband's survey regarding "What Women Want in a Man." Each chapter discusses one of the responses, prioritized from the least important quality listed to the most important quality in the survey answers. I have saved the quality most desired by women for last.

Each chapter will also contain a special section for men titled, "Hints for Him." These hints will aid a man to give a woman what she needs.

I will also include a section, "From Dr. Anne," in each chapter. Let me introduce Dr. Anne Reed to you. I am not a licensed marriage counselor. I can speak to you from personal experiences covering nearly twenty-nine years of marriage and my experience as a pastor's wife in a congregation of 18,000 members, including the research I have done for this book. Dr. Anne Reed will contribute additional information from a professional viewpoint. Dr. Anne is a vibrant and dedicated woman of God who counsels according to the Word of God. She received her bachelor of science in education and masters of business administration from Angelo State University in Texas. She did doctorate study at the University of Texas and received her PhD in counseling from the University of Amsterdam.

She has extensive experience in corporate as well as family counseling. Teaching, lecturing, and seminar development have been major scopes and missions for her ministry. Dr. Reed is presently a pastoral care counselor for Cornerstone Church in San Antonio, Texas, under the leadership of my husband and myself. Dr. Anne is dedicated to family reconciliation through healthy Christian spiritual values.

John and I entrust the sheep of our church to Dr. Anne with her skills and her knowledge of marriage relationships. This same trust is extended to the reader as you glean from her wisdom and advice. She will comment on each topic as if you were sitting on her counseling couch.

Scattered throughout each chapter will be a parallel thought from my husband's section of this book, titled, *What Every Man Wants in a Woman*. You will find similar comments from me scattered through the pages of his section of the book. These comments will be called "He Says..." in this section of the book and "She Says..." in my husband's section. As you read these parallel ideas, you will recognize clearly the differences in the way a man thinks from the way a woman thinks. They demonstrate the essence of this book—and these clearly recognizable differences are the reason why we thought it was important to write the book together.

Lastly and most importantly, each topic will end with a prayer of repentance for the things we have done wrong within our marriages and a prayer of new beginnings to enable us to start fresh in our quest to be the best we can be in our relationships with our loved ones and with our Father in heaven.

Repentance is the key to our salvation. Repentance is the key to growing in God. Repentance is a road we should walk often as we strive to be all we can be in Christ. Sadly, repentance is often the road less traveled by the men and women who enter into covenant with one another. It is my desire that by the time you finish reading this book, repentance will be second nature to you and that you will be longing for the good things of God.

Welcome to *What Every Woman Wants in a Man*. After you read this portion of the book written by me from my female point of view, be sure you flip over to my husband's portion, **What Every Man Wants in a Woman**.

The Scriptures dictate for us to put on the helmet of salvation so we can protect our minds from the fiery darts of the evil one. First Thessalonians tells us that the helmet of salvation is also the helmet of hope. The mind is the place where hope abides. Hope is a treasured gift of God. Hope is what enables us to face tomorrow with anticipation and joy. The Word of God states that Jesus Christ is our "blessed hope" (Titus 2:13). I want you to put on the helmet of hope every day and know that the One who holds your tomorrow also holds your marriage. To abide in Jesus Christ and in His Word, which are the manifestations of hope in this world, will make your marriage a sanctuary of heaven on earth, for as long as there is life there is hope.

one

Want Number Ten:
FAITHFULNESS

Most men will proclaim each his own goodness,
But who can find a faithful man?
The righteous man walks in his integrity;
His children are blessed after him.
                                        —PROVERBS 20:6–7

EVERY WOMAN WANTS to know, without a shadow of a doubt, that her boyfriend, fiancé, or spouse is completely loyal to her in thought and deed. One of the many reasons we, as believers, can have such unconditional trust in our Savior is because of His true faithfulness.

Therefore know that the LORD your God, He is God, the faithful God who keeps covenant and mercy for a thousand generations with those who love Him and keep His commandments.
                                        —DEUTERONOMY 7:9

The adjectives that describe a faithful person are *steadfast in affection or allegiance* or *loyal*. This man is firm in adherence to promises or in observance of duty or *conscientious*. A faithful individual is one who is given to assurance or one who is *bound by promise*.

If a woman says that she wants a faithful man, what she is really asking for is a man who will not have an affair and who will be loyally committed to her for life. She wants to trust him completely. That sounds simple enough. However, where two people are involved within a marriage relationship, there are several complex issues.

Nationally acclaimed clinical psychologist Dr. Willard F. Harley Jr., in his book *His Needs, Her Needs: Building an Affair-Proof Marriage,* refers to the high expectations men and women have for their marriages.[1] Both want their needs met, yet seldom do they communicate those needs to their spouse or take the time to know the needs of the other.

Dr. Harley states: "The main reason needs are often not met within the union of marriage is not selfish unwillingness to be considerate, but true ignorance of each other's needs."[2]

I have found that many individuals try to learn to "do without" having their needs met. They would rather do without than attempt to convey to their mate their true needs. There is no greater fear on earth than to stand emotionally naked before the one you love most in life, fearing that person will laugh at your desires or refuse to give you what you desperately want.

For example, a man who lists sexual fulfillment as one of his needs, and whose wife fulfills this need, makes his wife a continual source of intense pleasure, and his love for her grows stronger.

However, if this need is not met, he begins to associate her with frustration. Eventually, he will decide she "doesn't like sex." One of three things will happen: he will grin and bear it, or he will live a sexually frustrated life, or he will be unfaithful.

Adultery does not occur overnight. The man usually begins by conversing with a close female friend, someone at the office, or a neighbor. The "conversation only" friendship then develops into a deeper relationship of trust and desire. One step at a time the marriage is compromised by deeper feelings of trust and emotional dependence in the third party, and if he does not stop himself, adultery will result.

> **HE SAYS…**
> **When you buy a car, the car payment is the amount due. When you get married, sex is the payment of what is due.**

Not every man who is unfaithful in his marriage has a wife who does not fulfill his sexual or emotional needs. The rise of pornography and the casual attitude for marriage within the world have contributed greatly to the decline of fidelity within marriage. The word *vow* means little.

Former pastor Bob Moeller, in his book *For Better, For Worse, For Keeps*, makes the clever yet true statement: "If you keep your vows, they will keep your marriage."[3] A vow is a solemn promise made to

God—a promise of fidelity and love for the spouse you have chosen.

We as women need to understand the warning signs of a frustrated partner and turn to the Lord to make us all we can be within our marriage commitment.

We must ask ourselves these questions: What are my husband's needs? What am I doing to meet his needs? What am I doing to create frustration in him? Have I communicated to him what my sexual desires and needs are? What does the Word of God say about our sexual relationships? How can I change and be a better spouse?

There are certain biblical facts about sex that should be acknowledged:

1. Sex is God-given. Satan cannot offer anything in this realm other than distortion and emptiness. Sex was created by God to allow a husband and wife to express oneness through intimate and exclusive love. Our Creator designed sex to be pleasurable. Read Song of Solomon 4:1–16.

2. God created sex to be both a physical and a spiritual bond. He made two people out of one, and the two are not complete until they become one again through the sexual union within marriage.

And Adam said: "This is bone of my bones and flesh of my flesh; she shall be called Woman, because she was taken out of Man." Therefore a man shall leave his father and mother and be joined to his wife, and they shall become one flesh. And they were both naked, the man and his wife, and were not ashamed.

—GENESIS 2:23–24

3. God created sex to have purposeful boundaries. Anything outside of this total and exclusive covenant between husband and wife is destructive.

..."For this reason a man shall leave his father and mother and be joined to his wife, and the two shall become one flesh"? So then, they are no longer two but one flesh. Therefore what God has joined together, let not man separate.

—MATTHEW 19:5–6

4. The God-given purposes for sexual intimacy are these:

    a. *Unity*—"Man shall...be joined to his wife" (Gen. 2:24).

    b. *Comfort*—"Isaac...took Rebekah and she became his wife, and he loved her. So Isaac was comforted after his mother's death" (Gen. 24:67).

    c. *Procreation*—"Then God blessed them, and God said to them, 'Be fruitful and multiply'" (Gen. 1:28).

    d. *A defense against temptation*—"Nevertheless, because of sexual immorality, let each man have his own wife, and let each woman have her own husband....Do not deprive one another except with consent for a time...so that Satan does not tempt you because of your lack of self-control" (1 Cor. 7:2, 5).

    A husband is commanded to find satisfaction (Prov. 5:19) and joy (Eccles. 9:9) with his wife and to concern himself with meeting her unique needs (Deut. 24:5; 1 Pet. 3:7). A wife is responsible for availability (1 Cor. 7:3–5), preparation and planning (Song of Sol. 4:9), interest (Song of Sol. 4:16; 5:2), and sensitivity to her husband's needs (Gen. 24:67).[4]

When was the last time you created a romantic atmosphere for you and your husband? When was the last time you chose to meet his sexual desires? Have you even tried to meet them?

A man likes to be courted. He needs to be wanted. A phone call during the day that lets him know you are thinking of him in an intimate way will do wonders. He wants to know he is your hero. Buy, and wear, I might add, flattering nightgowns, and create a romantic atmosphere as often as possible.

When you and your husband find yourselves in an intimate moment, let him know exactly what you need and want from him within the confines of your bedroom. I know some of you are shaking your heads right now and thinking that your husband would probably have a heart attack if you did this. You have to start sometime, and the time is now!

What if you know what your husband's needs are, and you either refuse or can't meet his needs? What then?

To the woman who knows her husband's needs but refuses to meet them, Scripture states in 1 Corinthians 7:2–5:

> Nevertheless, because of sexual immorality, let each man have his own wife, and let each woman have her own husband. Let the husband render to his wife affection due her, and likewise also the wife to her husband. The wife does not have authority over her own body, but the husband does. And likewise the husband does not have authority over his own body, but the wife does. Do not deprive one another except with consent for a time, that you may give yourselves to fasting and prayer; and come together again so that Satan does not tempt you because of your lack of self-control.

The apostle Paul speaks about the importance of the sexual relationship between a man and his wife. This relationship is more than a biological requirement for reproducing. Marriage is the only location where God ordains sex. Within the confines of marriage the sexual union is a blessing. Outside, it is a cause for judgment.

HE SAYS . . .

God created Eve and brought her on His arm down the grassy slopes of the Garden of Eden. She was a perfect ten. She was absolutely naked and totally stunning. Adam started singing that well-known song "I Just Feel Like Something Good Is About to Happen."

Some of you may simply use sex within your marriage as a tool of manipulation. Manipulation is a sin and will destroy your marriage. When you send verbal and nonverbal signals to your husband that dictate to him what he will or will not receive based on what you get in return, you are practicing manipulation. I instruct you in one clear word, *STOP*! First of all, you are compromising a beautiful gift that God has made provision for within the sacrament of marriage. Second, you are riding for a fall. God is not a respecter of persons, and sooner or later you will pay the consequence for this action.

Some of you may have inhibitions regarding this intimate part of your marriage. In order to fulfill this requirement of marriage, you should seek direction from a professional Christian counselor. You owe this to yourself, your husband, and your marriage.

If you have a medical condition that prohibits you from providing a conventional sexual relationship for your husband, first seek medical advice, and then come into agreement with your husband as to how you can meet his physical needs. My husband and I highly recommend a book written by a Christian gynecologist, Dr. Scott Farhart, titled *Intimate and Unashamed*, which covers sexual topics from a clinical and biblical perspective.[5] You must learn to utilize all the godly tools available in order to have the best marriage relationship you can have.

Bob Moeller makes reference to "three true aphrodisiacs" of marriage. Moeller declares that no matter how beautiful or unattractive, old or young, every individual can possess love stimulants within their marriage.[6]

The first is *forgiveness*. When used, this ingredient can even change the chemical makeup of an individual. Why is there a sudden burst of sexual attraction when a couple has a fight and then reconciles? Our oneness established by our Creator has been restored, and we want to express this restoration through intimacy.

My husband often asks our congregation this question: "Do you want to be right or reconciled?" Ultimately, each individual must make this decision. Forgiveness is not a feeling we achieve but a choice we make. Granting forgiveness is not always easy. At times it is the hardest thing we will ever do.

To forgive someone we don't want to forgive, or to forgive someone who has not asked for forgiveness and has no repentant spirit, is not easy. We would rather bite our tongue in half. Many of my arguments with my husband have turned into arguments with the Lord.

"Lord, did You hear what he said to me?" "I can't believe he could even think that way about me!" "Me! The person who has always stood by him! Me! The person who is always trying to please him!"

"I'll tell you what, Lord; I'll forgive him if he admits he's been wrong *first*." "Lord, I don't want him to simply say he is sorry and think everything is all right! I want blood!"

The Lord then softly rebukes me and reminds me that it is not always about "me"! I have to listen to His voice and do what He asks and do it when He asks. Even when I don't want to, or don't feel that I should. Forgiveness is not conditional to our feelings but is determined by our obedience. When we extend forgiveness, we emulate our Savior. When we act like our Savior, it brings a smile to the face of God.

There were two couples in our church whose families had become close friends. Through circumstances not ordained by God, the husband of one family and the wife of the other began a torrid sexual affair. Once discovered, we immediately put both couples into counseling, each one proclaiming a desire for reconciliation. Time passed, and healing seemed to occur. More time passed, and the two resumed their affair. Discouraged, yet still hopeful because the offended parties desired to forgive, we led the two couples through counseling once again. However, this time we asked one of the families to leave the church in order to give both families a chance to survive.

The couple that stayed in the church began their road to recovery. The offended party had every biblical right to a divorce but chose for the life and not the death of the marriage. The road was long and steep. The road was often tiresome and tedious. But the path of repentance led to healing. This couple is now a prime example of true forgiveness and restoration, and now offers help to those who find themselves in similar situations. This couple is able to give back to others what God has given them—grace, mercy, and restoration.

The couple that left our church continued down the path of destruction with a pattern of infidelity and forgiveness, infidelity and forgiveness. The Word of God sets before us life and death, blessings and curses. We must choose. Sadly, both husband and wife enabled the other to continue the path of death for their marriage.

My husband tells our sheep that to "extend forgiveness without demanding change makes the grace of God an accomplice to evil." Change is a condition that makes forgiveness a divine tool in the hands of the believer.

To make mistakes is part of our human nature, but to institutionalize those mistakes and make them part of our personality and character is to deny the image of Jesus Christ in which we were created. Asking forgiveness cancels out the past because of the blood covering of our Lord and Savior. This is one of the pillars of our faith through which we can begin anew and free ourselves from the bondage of our past. If we can ask for forgiveness, then we must extend forgiveness.

Moeller states that forgiveness is an act of our will that releases others from the moral debt they owe us.[7] Forgiveness is not given because it is earned or deserved, but because it's needed. Forgiveness is mercy, not justice. We must learn to extend forgiveness as our Creator extended it to us. His whole nature is forgiving.

The second aphrodisiac is *surrender*. Because of cultural, moral, and generational differences, we all bring fears, insecurities, and inhibitions into our marriages. Moeller states that the level of intimacy and vulnerability that our Creator designed into the sexual union forces these hidden feelings to surface.[8] My husband often tells his congregation that legalism dictates, "If it feels good, then it must be sin!" This doctrine has caused many Christians to believe that enjoying sex is wrong.

God intended the sexual union within marriage to be a source of blessing, enjoyment, and joy for the husband and the wife. When we surrender our lives to God, we miraculously get our lives back to do His will and accomplish all He purposes for us. This action also applies to our marriages. To surrender all is frightening, but it is the only way to maximize our return.

The feminist movement equates surrender with losing one's identity. Nothing could be further from the truth. We do not become a slave to our partner when we surrender to him, and we do not give away our individualism, uniqueness, or dignity.

Surrender within marriage simply means voluntarily yielding ourselves to one another in love. Surrender is letting go of the fears and inhibitions of the past that have caused walls to come between you and your husband, and yielding to the concept that God has ordained the two of you to "become one flesh." Surrender is not weakness. Surrender takes strength and character.

The third aphrodisiac is *unselfishness*. *Making love* is much more than the sexual act. Romance is a great part of the sexual union. Dr. Farhart details the biological differences of men and women in the sexual realm. He discusses the human anatomy and the miraculous way it was constructed by the Creator and why it is we respond so differently to sexual intercourse.[9] It is important for us to have this knowledge, for it is not simply the truth that will set us free but the "knowledge" of the truth that will set us free from the bondages of cross locker-room talk and old wives' tales.

Moeller describes simply the sexual differences between a man and a woman by comparing them to a race car and a freight train. The race car is revved and ready to go. It gets to the goal fast and stops abruptly.

The freight train begins slow, yet eventually and powerfully it gets to its destination and slowly comes to a stop.[10]

It is evident that both partners must be sensitive to each other's needs and be willing to give unselfishly of themselves in order to fulfill the desires of the other. Even the simplest rules, like agreeing not to use the marriage bed to talk about family or business, can add pleasure to your time together. Communicate to your husband that there is nothing more important than your time of intimacy with him.

The world has kept the believer in "secular darkness" long enough. We must let the "Light of the world," Jesus Christ, bring enlightenment to every part of our lives, including our sexual relationships with our spouse.

Women read romance novels and love to go to *chick flicks* because of the tender affection that is shown the heroine. Lovemaking for the woman begins with holding hands and hugs, love pats and compliments. It doesn't begin when the lights go out and the door is locked.

For the man, true lovemaking and satisfaction also include knowing that he is wanted and needed. Your husband's satisfaction and desire are multiplied when he knows he is a hero in your life. Learn to give of yourself unselfishly. There is no greater satisfaction within the sexual act than to know that you have pleased the one you love.

Intimacy is not a formula—it's a way of life.

HINTS FOR HIM

Yearn to be faithful. Strive to be faithful. Be faithful in thought and deed. This is not only a character trait that a woman wants in a man, but it is also a trait that God wants in His people. He rewards faithfulness. (See Proverbs 28:20; Matthew 25:14–30.) Faithfulness is part of a solid foundation for every successful marriage.

A woman wants a man who will commit to his marriage for the long haul. She wants a man who wants to be a loyal husband and values this loyalty as a cornerstone for a healthy marriage.

Listen. A woman wants more than what you are hearing coming from her mouth. Learn to listen to all of her.

Let her know that she is what you want in life and that there is no one else who could satisfy you as she does. Hold her, and tell her you love her.

Finally, learn to communicate your needs and desires to your wife so she has the opportunity to meet every need you have. Make your intimate time together precious and pure.

FROM DR. ANNE

A faithful husband is a blessing from God. How can you have that blessing, and what do we really mean by the term *faithful*? Faithfulness comes when you have a relationship that is truly blessed and a marriage that is consecrated and holy. There is never a doubt of loyalty in that atmosphere. Your husband will be worthy of being believed in word and deed. He will consider you a blessing. He will be steadfast in the covenant he has made with you. You'll never have a need for suspicion or mistrust in an atmosphere of faithfulness.

Here comes the problem. The man I have just described deserves to have a woman with those same qualities. In fact, unless you have those attributes, I can promise you that anything you say to influence your husband will fall on deaf ears.

This is not a book for the rebellious woman who has no intention of changing. Submission to God's Word is required for you to enjoy the blessings that you say you want. You get what you give. God says that He will use the same measuring cup we use to give to others to give back to us (Matt. 7:2). Your degree of faithfulness and loving submission will influence the faithfulness of your husband.

How can you be faithful? Are you faithful to remember the very simple things that you want your husband to be faithful to? Do you remember birthdays, anniversaries, and milestones in your relationship? Do you follow through with the commitment to do what you have agreed to do?

Take a serious look at how you act and how much your mind is subjected to the Holy Spirit. Do you have thoughts about other men? Do you dress, act, or talk in a seductive way? Do you remain faithful to the plans and hopes that you have made with your husband? Do you embellish or lie when the truth is required? How many times have you told a half-truth to justify something to your husband? How many times have you colored your actions because you knew he would disapprove?

Have you considered how your husband would react if he found out that you were talking to or contacting an old boyfriend? What about chat rooms? What about e-mail? How important is it that you please another person more than your husband? How faithful are you?

Are you the wife that can be "faithful" to administer comfort and nurture your husband in times of need? Give what you want to receive.

Your hope for all things is in prayer alone. I pray that you are not involved in any of these things. If you are, *stop it!* Learn to pray for your husband to your Father God. Don't pray *at him*. Learn to pray blessings on your husband. Speak love and encouragement. You don't have to tattle to God about what your husband is doing. God already knows.

CLOSING PRAYERS

Our Creator is the source of our blessings, and as you turn to Him and His Word for direction, you will find Him ever faithful. Forgiveness, surrender, and unselfishness are three powerful traits given to you by God. These ingredients are ordained by Him to create deep, intimate, and loving relationships. When you offer these three elements to your mate in love and sincerity, they become the foundation to irresistible love.

PRAYER OF REPENTANCE

Father, forgive me. Like David, I have sinned before You and You alone. I come to You with a repentant heart. Forgive me for the times I have been unfaithful to my husband in my thoughts and in my actions toward him. Forgive me for the times I have rejected him when he was trying to share his inner thoughts and desires with me. Forgive me, Lord, for knowing what he needed and wanted and intentionally not providing. Forgive me for giving my best to others while taking my husband for granted. I have flirted with ideas that would hurt my husband deeply. In hurting him, I have hurt You, and I am truly sorry and ask Your forgiveness.

PRAYER OF NEW BEGINNINGS

Precious Father God, I am so thankful that You gave me Your Son, Jesus. He is the greatest example of faithfulness. He never swerved in His loyalty to You. He never looked aside from the plan You had set before Him.

Father, I thank You for the life You have given me with my husband. I thank You that we are both committed to You and to our marriage. I will be faithful to him in everything I say and do. I will not be tempted to open the door of disloyalty. With Your help I will strive to bless my husband daily and do all I can to make our home heaven on earth. Our children will see our marriage and want what we have. I will live my life and think my thoughts according to Your Word. I don't want to grieve the Holy Spirit with disobedience, thereby displeasing my Creator and Savior. Thank You, Lord, for being a God of new beginnings. Thank You for giving to me the man You want me to have so we may serve You all the days of our lives. Amen.

two

Want Number Nine:
LEADERSHIP

> For the husband is head of the wife, as also Christ
> is head of the church; and He is the Savior of the
> body.
>
> —EPHESIANS 5:23

A WOMAN WANTS A man to know who he is, to know where he is going, and to know how he is going to get there. She wants a man with confidence in himself, in her, and in their relationship. She wants him to lead her and her children with kindness and understanding. She wants him to be firm, yet gentle. She wants him to consult the Lord and her before any major decision is made to insure that he makes the right decision at all times.

Wow! Who can find such a man? His worth is more than all the riches of the world! Actually, this man is probably living with you right now. The question is not *Who can find him?* but *How can I, as his wife, help him to become this leader?*

My husband often says, "For every crooked pot there is a crooked lid!" In observing a diversity of relationships, I have sadly come to the conclusion that some pots don't have lids that fit. In my prayer time for these sheep, I often find myself trying to make a deal with God: "Lord, wouldn't it be perfect if this lid went with that pot?" Or, "How nice it would be for that lid to go with this pot. Life would be more fair and much nicer."

Then, of course, I come to my senses and realize that perfection is attained *in the world to come*—not in this life. In this world, we must walk by the law of God's Word and by the grace of His cross. Only the

Master Potter can mold each of us into the design He wants and make every lid fit perfectly with every pot. To have a "perfect fit" we must let Him work His plan.

There is a perfect plan designed by our Creator. God has placed divinely ordained traits within each one of us that, if activated, will allow His plan to work. However, so often in our human quest for power over our natural world, we forget God's design. Therefore we erect barriers that prevent His plan from transforming our marriage relationships into God's design.

Our quest for power often causes power struggles in our marriages. Noted anthropologist Margaret Mead asked a very important question regarding our society and the role reversal of the sexes: "Have we over-domesticated men?...Have we cut women off from their natural closeness to their children, taught them to look for a job instead of the touch of a child's hand?...All this in the name of equality?"[1]

The struggle for power has existed long before the desire for equality between man and woman. From the time in the garden, woman has tried to override man's leadership. Eve did not force Adam to take the apple; it happened more like this:

> The night is cool and beautiful by the light of the full moon. You can hear the owls serenade the evening as the wind rustles gently through the lush green leaves of the majestic trees set on the horizon. The sweet fragrance of honeysuckle fills the air. Life is good.
>
> Eve is adorned in nothing but a soft smile and anticipation as she awaits her husband's arrival from a stroll in the garden. Adam has been taking inventory over his entire domain. He sees his wife dressed in desire. The table is set with a splendid meal. Breathless, he admires her incomparable beauty. (So whom could he compare her to?) Oh, what a night this will be.
>
> There is a new recipe on the menu: fruit salad. This dish has a new ingredient: apples. She would not have been so bold as to make such a forbidden course if a slithering traveling salesman had not come calling while Adam was out. He peddled his wares, and Eve bought them. "To have knowledge and wisdom is to have power," the serpent convincingly persuaded her. Dinner is served.

You know the rest of the story. We ate ourselves out of paradise. Today is no different.

One day my husband came home from work and was rather frustrated. It had been a very bad day for him. Little was accomplished, and he was aggravated beyond words when he walked through the door. I have learned to read him well. His eyes were glazed, his jaw set, and his tongue rolled in his mouth. I was making dinner, and there was little I could say that would calm him down from the day's disappointments.

"Adam was so stupid! He listened to that silly woman and ate that dumb apple! If it wasn't for him, we would still be in paradise and not have to work for a living and put up with all this nonsense!" he ranted.

I tried to get a word in edgewise, but nothing would do. Finally, a bit perturbed at him by now, I continued to carefully peel the beautiful red apple I was holding. As I listened to his litany of complaints, I methodically sliced the apple and gently enticed him to open his mouth. Without thinking, he paused momentarily to bite down on the sweet-tasting offering I held in my hand. I watched him as he chewed with satisfaction and swallowed my tasty trap.

"There, if it had not been Adam, it would have been you!" I proudly announced, having proven my point. With that said, he almost threw up my illustrated sermon. He did not appreciate my object lesson. It was a long night.

In order to be a leader, you must have someone to lead. A woman wants her husband to lead; however, we must remember that it is our responsibility to submit to his leadership. And there, my friends, lies the rub.

As I was praying for direction on a topic for a Bible study for our women's class, I felt the Lord leading me to teach on submission. I knew it had to be the Lord's direction, because this was not a topic I was passionate about. I announced the class, and very few women signed up. Later, at the prodding of my peers, I renamed the class, "Submission, and How I Conquered It!" Surprisingly, the class immediately filled, and I began to teach the "S" word.

One of the first questions I asked the women was: "How many of you have no trouble submitting to your husband?" Several women raised their hands. Much to their dismay, I responded to their raised hands with this statement: "If you have no trouble submitting, then you have never truly submitted."

Submission is one of the most difficult actions you will ever undertake as a Christian woman. It is a difficult task. And if not done under

God's empowerment, it is downright impossible! True submission occurs when you follow your spiritual authority's lead, even when every fiber in you feels it's the wrong path to take. And you must do this in a willing and respectful way. Comedienne Rita Rudner gave her opinion on submission: "When I eventually met *Mr. Right*, I had no idea his first name was *Always*."

Submission is a *mandate*, not a suggestion.

> In like manner, you married women, be submissive to your husbands [subordinate yourselves as being secondary to and dependent on them, and adapt yourselves to them], so that even if any do not obey the Word [of God], they may be won over not by discussion but by the [godly] lives of their wives. When they observe the pure and modest way in which you conduct yourselves, together with your reverence [for your husband; you are to feel for him all that reverence includes: to respect, defer to, revere him—to honor, esteem, appreciate, prize, and, in the human sense, to adore him, that is, to admire, praise, be devoted to, deeply love, and enjoy your husband]. Let not yours be the [merely] external adorning with [elaborate] interweaving and knotting of the hair, the wearing of jewelry, or changes of clothes; but let it be the inward adorning and beauty of the hidden person of the heart, with the incorruptible and unfading charm of a gentle and peaceful spirit, which [is not anxious or wrought up, but] is very precious in the sight of God.
> —1 PETER 3:1–4, AMP

This scripture lists three main reasons why wives should submit to their husbands:

1. In obedience to the Word of God
2. To bring the lost to the saving knowledge of Jesus Christ
3. To be precious in the eyes of God

These should be sufficient reasons to submit, and to do so in a sweet spirit.

Not hardly! By the very nature of the word, *submission* means "to capitulate to another's desires, to surrender one's will, to give in, to acquiesce to someone else's lead." The antonym of submission is *resistance*. I

HE SAYS ...

The Bible says, "For the husband is head of the wife" (Eph. 5:23). God is not in heaven saying, "Let's make a deal!" He's in heaven saying, "This is the deal!"

find that the "R" word is something women practice much more than the "S" word.

SUBMISSION SECRETS

There are a couple of *submission secrets* I will share with you in order to give you a fair opportunity to successfully accomplish this God-ordained mandate.

Submission is not an act of the will; it is a condition of the heart.

It is fruitless to try and submit your carnal will to that of your husband's. It is the nature of man to win. To attempt to submit "flesh to flesh" is like getting a root canal without an anesthetic. It makes an awful noise and is so painful you don't want to do it often.

Love does not measure success by strong will—tallying who gets his or her way. To the contrary, to love as Christ loves is to give—to give of yourself to the other in such a way that pleases the Creator and the person with whom you have decided to spend the rest of your life. If you live to please a man, you will never please your Father in heaven. In contrast, if you live to please your Father in heaven, then you can please the man you marry.

You must submit to God before you can submit to any man.

I compare this action to that of a satellite uplink. Imagine your husband asking you to follow his direction. You think about it. *Nope! Over my dead body!* is your first thought.

Having wisely decided not to voice your instinctive opinion, you ask God for help. In desperation you look upward. You "link" to Him in the heavenlies.

His Spirit becomes your spirit. Somehow, you suddenly have a change of thought. You realize that if you do your part as the Master Potter mandates, then He will cover you and honor your obedient action.

But wait a minute; there's more. Your second instinct is to say something like, "Well, OK, but I want you to know that I am only doing this your way because the Lord wants me to, and since I am such a 'spirrrritual' person I will do as you ask. Even though I feel this is the most stupid decision you have ever made!"

Wrong! Satisfying, but wrong. You look up again and ask the Father to renew your mind and create in you a willing and sweet spirit. This task takes a little longer to accomplish, usually determined by the hormonal readings of the moment. I might warn you at this point...since I am in the sisterhood of women, submission never comes at the right time.

The uplink is complete. Now for the downlink. You look at your husband and assure him that you love him. "I know that leading me and our children takes great wisdom and responsibility," you tell him. "I will follow your lead as I pray for God to give you direction and discernment."

It's now complete. The mandate is accomplished. The Lord is pleased. Your husband is shocked. And you will be blessed no matter what the outcome.

We all have heard the phrase "a woman's place." Our Creator has a special place for us. When God puts a woman *in her place*, it is a place of honor, a high and lofty place. When this carnal world puts a woman in her place, it is usually a demeaning place far lower than what our Lord has destined for us to have.

In order to be right where God wants you to be, you must be obedient to His Word. Deuteronomy 28:1–2 tells us that if we heed His voice and obey His commandments, He will cause His blessings to overtake us. I love the sound of that. He will cause His blessings to "overtake us." This means that whether we think we deserve it or not, He will bless us. But first we must obey.

In his book *Spiritual Authority,* Watchman Nee states that to be filled with Christ is to be filled with obedience. Since the Lord initiated obedience, the Father has become the head of Christ. Since God has instituted both authority and obedience, it is natural for those who know God and Christ to obey. Those who know not God and Christ know neither authority nor obedience. Christ is the principle of obedience. Therefore a person who is filled with Christ must be filled with obedience.[2]

God sets up His authority in the home. Throughout His Word we see the pattern of familial authority. To rebel against this divinely appointed authority is to rebel against the kingdom ordained by God Himself. God has set the husband as the delegated authority of Christ, with the wife as representative of the church. It is difficult for the wife to be subject to her husband if she does not realize that the real issue is *God's authority*, not her husband's:

That they may encourage the young women to love their husbands, to love their children, to be sensible, pure, workers at home, kind, being subject to their own husbands, that the word of God may not be dishonored.

—TITUS 2:4–5, NAS

My position on this subject is simple: I want God's blessing on my life! I don't want to be guilty of blaspheming God's Word! What must I do to qualify for His blessing? The answer is *to obey*!

As you learn to obey God's instruction to be submissive to your husband, you can help him to become an effective and godly leader. The following ten things will help you to do that:

1. *Respect him.* Show honor and reverence to him in your home and to your friends and family. "Likewise, their wives must be reverent, not slanderers, temperate, faithful in all things" (1 Tim. 3:11).

2. *Acknowledge his calling as the high priest of your home.* Don't try to override his authority with your children in the spirit of Absalom. "Oh, that I were made judge in the land...I would give him justice" (2 Sam. 15:4).

3. *Respond to his leadership.* Don't tell him you will follow him and then do your own thing. You may deceive your husband for a season, but you won't fool the Lord for a second. "For the word of God is living and powerful, and sharper than any two-edged sword, piercing even to the division of soul and spirit, and of joints and marrow, and is a discerner of the thoughts and intents of the heart" (Heb. 4:12).

4. *Praise him.* Women do not realize that a man needs praise just as often as a woman needs it. Praise your husband for providing for your home and family and for leading you in the ways of the Lord. "...and let the wife see that she respects and reverences her husband [that she notices him, regards him, honors him, prefers him, venerates, and

esteems him; and that she defers to him, praises him, and loves and admires him exceedingly]" (Eph. 5:33, AMP).

5. *Be unified with him in purpose and in will.* When you come together as one in your goals and your supplications, God acknowledges your unity, and He grants your petitions. "Can two walk together, except they be agreed?" (Amos 3:3, KJV).

6. *Be his helpmate.* Don't compete with your husband. Learn to complement him. "Now the Lord God said, It is not good (sufficient, satisfactory) that the man should be alone; I will make him a helper meet (suitable, adapted, complementary) for him" (Gen. 2:19, AMP).

7. *Listen to him.* Don't be the mouth of the body when God is calling you to be the ear and heart of the body. The ancient prophet prayed, "Give unto me, O Lord, a hearing heart." Proverbs 4:4 says, "He taught me and said to me, Let your heart hold fast my words; keep my commandments and live" (AMP).

8. *Pray with him and for him.* It is so important that God hear your petitions for your husband. Cover him in prayer daily, praying that discernment and wisdom will guide him. "And pray in the Spirit on all occasions with all kinds of prayers and requests. With this in mind, be alert and always keep on praying for all the saints" (Eph. 6:18, NIV).

9. *Bless him.* I try to bless my husband every day before he leaves our home. There is a battlefield outside of the doors of our home, and he needs all the help he can get. The power of the blessing provides a blanket of protection and favor. "The LORD bless thee, and keep thee: The LORD make his face shine upon thee, and be gracious unto thee: The LORD lift up his countenance upon thee, and give thee peace. And they shall put my name upon the children of Israel; and I will bless them" (Num. 6:24–27, KJV).

10. *Be thankful for him.* So many women do not realize the gift their husband truly is until they lose him. Thank the Lord every day for your husband, and call out in him the traits that God wants in him to be the man He has destined him to be. "I thank my God always concerning you for the grace of God which was given to you by Christ Jesus, that you were enriched in everything by Him in all utterance and all knowledge, even as the testimony of Christ was confirmed in you, so that you come short in no gift, eagerly waiting for the revelation of our Lord Jesus Christ, who will also confirm you to the end, that you may be blameless in the day of our Lord Jesus Christ" (1 Cor. 1:4–8).

THE IMPORTANCE OF TRUSTING

I want to talk to you about trust for a moment. It is critical for you to know, without question, that you can trust God with your life, with your husband's life, and with the lives of your family members. Make the decision once and for all that you will trust that God loves you and wants only what is best for you.

God *IS* trustworthy. Everything about Him is trustworthy. He is enough for every problem, and His power and wisdom will care for your every concern. Your trust in God is *your strength*.

This trust brings out the best in you as a woman, as a wife, and as a mother.

Once a woman puts her trust in God, then she can put her trust in her husband, but not until then. Without this trust, unity within marriage will not be possible. In their book *10 Weeks to a Better Marriage*, Randall and Therese Cirner refer to a friend of theirs who told them, "God I can trust! He's perfect. But my husband...that's another story! I know he makes mistakes!"[3]

They list the following reasons women give for not trusting their husbands:

1. "He is not spiritual enough," *or* "I have been a Christian longer than he has."

2. "He still has faults," *or* "I'll trust him when he is perfect."

3. "He has made mistakes with our life in the past," *or* "How can I ever trust him again?"

4. "I'm better at decision making than he is," *or* "I know that I am right and he is wrong."

5. "I've been hurt so many times before in my past that I can't open myself to trust anyone again," *or* "Both my father and my husband disappointed me; I can never trust men again."[4]

What are the reasons you give for not trusting God or for not trusting your husband? Are they really reasons, or are they just *excuses*? Be aware that we sometimes try to avoid doing what is right by giving excuses for why we can't do what is expected of us in God's Word. Is that true of you? How can you change this cycle?

Most women have a very strong drive to lead. We like control because it gives us security. When my husband and I fly around the country, I always seem to worry about our safety. John always assures me that it safer to fly in a plane than to drive a car. But I always tell him that when I am in the air I am not in charge, but when I am driving the car I feel that I have more control of my life. I feel more self-assured when I am driving. It's all about control.

On one occasion we were flying by private charter on a plane that required a pilot and a copilot. I was reading a book when I realized the pilot was right in front of me, asking if all was well. Startled, I looked at the empty captain's seat and loudly asked the question, "Excuse me! But who is flying this plane?"

"The copilot is watching the instruments, and we are on autopilot. Everything is under control," the captain answered as he tried to assure me.

After I *assured* him that I did not like an empty pilot's seat, he took his rightful place. And I had to *trust* that he was in control.

> **HE SAYS . . .**
> **How sad that we spend so many years training for a career and so little time preparing for marriage.**

God is our pilot. He is in control. He instructs our husbands in the copilot's seat. Then there is the Holy Spirit, the autopilot, who makes sure everything is in complete harmony and balance.

As wives, we simply must trust. We must let go. We must let go of being right, let go of being more spiritual, let go of being hurt, let go of analyzing our husband's faults. We must let go of trying to be in total control of every situation and let God have His sovereign way in our lives and in our marriages.

HINTS FOR HIM

My husband often tells the men of our church, "It's hard to follow a parked car!" A woman wants her husband to take the lead of their household. This can be harmonious only when the husband is also submitted to the Lord as his Savior.

Watchman Nee states that while the Bible teaches that wives should be subject to their husbands, it also instructs that husbands should exercise authority with a condition. Husbands are called upon to love their wives as they love themselves three different times in Ephesians 5. Undoubtedly there is authority in the family. However, those in authority need to fulfill God's requirement. The love of Christ for the church sets the example for the love that a husband ought to give to his own wife. The love of a husband ought to be the same as the love of Christ for His church. If husbands wish to represent God's authority, they must love their wives so much that they are willing to die for them.

Another wise thought my husband gives both men and women regarding the topics of leadership and submission is this: "Wives, follow your husband's lead, and husbands, meet your wife's need." It is the responsibility of the husband to know what his wife's true needs are and to meet those needs to the best of his ability with joy and kindness.

You will never be a successful husband and father if you do not submit yourself to the authority of God the Father and of Jesus Christ His Son. If you are a man who is reading this book, I encourage you to live according to the Word of God. Ask God for direction and wisdom in the leadership role He has assigned to you. Remember this truth: God will equip you to do those things He has ordained you to do.

FROM DR. ANNE

Security and freedom belong to the woman who has a husband who is willing, able, and capable of taking the lead in the relationship she has with him. This godly man uses wisdom to lead his family, *not muscle*. Ideally, a woman wants her husband to lead with compassion and kindness, and he leads with a flexibility and desirability that is pleasing to the wife and brings smiles to the faces of his beloved children. In other words, he does exactly what the rest of the family wants and what agrees with the flow of the moment.

But it's not that simple! The ultimate security a woman desires in her marriage, *more than any other thing in marriage*, is rewarded to her *only* when she is supportive of her husband. Her confidence in his ability to make good decisions will reflect her confidence in him as a husband, father, and, ultimately, as a man. You have great power in your hands, either to encourage God's perfect will or to crush your husband's self-esteem and self-worth. Use this power wisely.

In the Christian home the family should follow the leader willingly. The Christian father and husband should not find it necessary to *force* his family to be obedient. A godly leader exhibits a stillness, maturity, and determination to follow the will of God for himself—and for his family. He must hear God clearly and follow God fully. If he can be dissuaded from the decision that God has made clear to him, then he lacks the consistency and obedience that God requires.

Do not be a woman who wants to take this leadership from your husband. I would be quick to tell you that there is a price to be paid. What good is a leader without anyone to lead? What if those he has been put in charge of refuse to be led? If a leader is not able to lead, out of frustration he will lose motivation and finally stop attempting to lead.

Your input is needed for your husband to make an educated move. How can any leader make an educated, wise decision without all the facts? However, your input is required only once! Continued input is otherwise known by the term *nagging*.

When a decision that your husband made turns out to be one that doesn't work very well, don't humiliate him by reminding him as often as possible that he really "blew it." Proverbs 14:1 says, "The wise woman builds her house, but the foolish pulls it down with her hands." Don't embarrass him by sharing his decision—and the outcome—with your children, his co-workers, and church friends.

God is such a wise instructor. In a very simple way, He will show you how to add strength and honor to your husband as he stands erect and tall in his role. Words of encouragement roll off the tongue so much easier than bitterness. Support can make a situation that is less than ideal easier to live with.

Join your husband in oneness, and make a solid stand together. Ask his opinions. Include him in your family discussions so he can have input that will help the process of leadership. Pray for your husband daily—continually! Prayer is the best support you can give to your husband and to your family. Through prayer, your husband will have the wisdom God wants him to use as he makes his decisions. Prayer never fails, because our God *NEVER* fails.

CLOSING PRAYERS

God created women to give life to those with whom we come in contact! In this chapter, I have helped you to recognize your importance in bringing life to your husband and family by your godly support and prayers. The life you give is *God's life*. If your husband is not yet a Christian, through your submissive attitude you have the power to give eternal life to him by leading him to Christ "without a word" (1 Pet. 3:2).

You have also learned that you can give life to your marriage by submitting to your husband as Christ your Savior submitted to His Father on the cross. By obeying the Word of God in submission, you will give your marriage new breath. Your marriage relationship will become an eternal blessing—one that you begin experiencing *right now!*

PRAYER OF REPENTANCE

Father, in the name of Your Son, Jesus, I ask You to forgive me for insisting on being right at the expense of my husband's dignity and self-respect. I repent sorrowfully. I am truly ashamed of my actions. Father God, in Jesus' name, I ask that You forgive me for undermining my husband's authority. I am so sorry for going behind his back and allowing our children to disobey their father's instructions. I am grieved that I didn't listen to his advice and did my own thing. My heart is truly heavy. I repent of the times I have used manipulation, domination, and intimidation to get my way. I know that I have sinned against my husband and grieved the Holy Spirit. I ask for Your forgiveness and Your mercy.

PRAYER OF NEW BEGINNINGS

My precious Father, I thank You for all the gifts that You have given me. I am truly blessed of You. I dedicate myself, my husband, and our children to You with the same love You showed us when you gave us Your only Son. I thank You for giving me a husband who loves me as Christ loves His church. I thank You for giving me a husband who shows compassion and understanding as he instructs our children. I accept the blessings that are mine as I walk in submission to You and to my husband. My husband grows in wisdom daily, and we are of one spirit. I want Your blessings and Your favor, which come from hearing Your voice and obeying Your Word. Amen.

three

Want Number Eight:
RESPECT

Come, you children, listen to me; I will teach you to revere and worshipfully fear the Lord. What man is he who desires life and longs for many days, that he may see good? Keep your tongue from evil and your lips from speaking deceit. Depart from evil and do good; seek, inquire for, and crave peace and pursue (go after) it!

—PSALM 34:11–14, AMP

However, let each man of you [without exception] love his wife as [being in a sense] his very own self; and let the wife see that she respects and reverences her husband [that she notices him, regards him, honors him, prefers him, venerates, and esteems him; and that she defers to him, praises him, and loves and admires him exceedingly].

—EPHESIANS 5:33, AMP

THE DEFINITION OF *respect* is, "to feel or show honor for; to think highly of; to look up to; to have polite regard and to be thoughtful and show kind consideration and concern for another individual." Every human being—man or woman—desires respect.

There is an element of dignity that is linked to the measure of respect we receive from others. The whole world around us can show an ultimate measure of respect for us, but if the person whom we love the most does not give us respect, we suffer from the lack of it.

Respect comes in two forms. The first form of respect is a form of regard that is shown for *the position* held by an individual. As wives we should respect the position of husband, father, and priest. As a husband, he should show respect for the position of woman, wife, and mother.

The Word of God is very clear that wives should show their respect for their husbands through submission to their authority. We are to respect our husband's role as father by not usurping his headship over the family.

We are to respect his role as the spiritual head of our household by holding him up in prayer and by having high regard for his leadership.

The Word of God is equally clear that the husband is to respect his wife. Our Creator places woman on a lofty pedestal. Christ says that a husband should love and respect his wife and the mother who brings his children into the world as Christ loves and respects His church. This we do in obedience to the Lord and His Word.

The second form of respect is much more valuable. This form of respect is linked to more than obedience. This form of respect is linked to *the person* and is expressed with love, trust, and gratitude.

Respect at this level is earned. A cardinal rule to follow when desiring this treasured form of respect is to give equal amounts of it away. As wives, before we can ask for respect from our husbands, we must first give respect to our husbands. I have found that some women demand respect for the positions they hold, but they are not as concerned about receiving respect from the hearts of the men who love them most, which is so much more valuable.

> **HE SAYS...**
>
> **Remember that your husband has a God-given role as leader of your home. Allow the Holy Spirit to help you willingly submit to his loving, godly leadership.**

This second level of respect, which is a beautiful expression of love and devotion, is the form of respect I will be referring to in the following pages. Before you can show any form of gratitude to your husband, you must first show it to the Lord, who gives you every perfect gift that comes from above.

> Enter into His gates with thanksgiving and a thank offering and into His courts with praise! Be thankful and say so to Him, bless and affectionately praise His name!
>
> —PSALM 100:4, AMP

THE COMPONENT OF GRATITUDE

Rebbetzin Jungreis describes one of the main components of respect. It's called *gratitude*. Gratitude is one of the pillars of Judaism and Christianity. For believers of Judaism, from the moment they wake in the morning to the time they go to sleep at night, they are called upon to declare praise and thanksgiving unto God. Rebbetzin says, "Our first words must be a proclamation of appreciation to the Almighty for having returned our souls and given us yet another day. No aspect of life is to be taken for granted—a glass of water, a tree in bloom, the rainbow in the sky must all be acknowledged with a blessing to God."[1]

The Jews proclaim praise unto God because they are commanded to praise Him. As Christians we must do the same, but we must also go one step further because of the cross of Christ and what our Savior did for us on that cross. We should praise Him out of relationship. We should praise Him out of love. When we exercise this form of praise for our Creator, then there is no time for complaints, murmuring, or depression. We will have less chance to take His bountiful blessings for granted.

When is the last time you said *thank you* to the Lord? At times you may feel you have nothing to be thankful for, but this is simply not the case. Everything that is good comes from God. Everything that is of value, like the breath in your lungs and the sight for your eyes, all the beauty that surrounds you comes from God. You should thank Him every moment that you can. To know that the God who created the universe is the same God who inhabits the praises of His people is reason enough to praise Him.

Not to have gratitude for the things of God is the beginning of self-destruction in your walk with God. You have a choice—to focus on the things you lack, or to give praises unto God for the constant blessings that are upon you every day. When you focus on the things you lack, you will always want for more, even when you receive what you want. You will see God through a "What have You done for me lately?" attitude. When you focus on the blessings of God with an *attitude of gratitude,* then your life begins to reach for the destiny He has ordained for you.

Once you learn to express your gratitude to the almighty God who created you, to His Son who died for you, and to His Holy Spirit who guides you, then you can express your gratitude to your husband. Begin this expression of gratitude with two very important words: "Thank you."

Rebbetzin breaks down the word *modim* or *thank you* in Hebrew to give us a greater understanding of what this phrase should mean in our lives. *Modim* or *thank you* has two connotations. *Thank you* also means, "to admit." In essence, "thank you" is an admission that you are in need, that you are vulnerable, that you cannot do it alone—and that admission is something that most of us do not like to concede. We hate feeling indebted, especially if the favor extended to us was significant. Therefore the greater the kindness and the closer the relationship, then the greater our reluctance to reveal our weakness by pronouncing those two little words. People who have no problem saying "Thank you" to a waiter in a restaurant, a telephone operator, or a salesperson have difficulty saying those same words to the people who are nearest and dearest because "Thank you" to them would be an admission of need.[2]

When is the last time you said "Thank you" to your husband? "For what?" you might ask. *For much.* He chose you as that special person with whom he passionately desires to spend the rest of his life. He helps to provide for you. The children whom you cherish are products of the love you share with him. Together, you go to the throne of God in prayer to give thanks and to petition the King of kings and the Lord of lords for your needs. Thank him often for being in your life.

I can't thank him, you may be thinking right now. *I don't have the kind of husband you just described.* Remember that faith is the assurance or confirmation of the things you hope for, being the proof of things you do not see, and the conviction of their reality. I know that you want the husband I described. You need to begin to thank the Lord for him, and thank your husband. Then watch him as he begins to change for the good. I believe it is your husband's ultimate desire to please you and his Savior, but often he lacks the knowledge of how to do so. You can begin to show him the way by showing respect and gratitude for the husband God has given you. Let God do the rest.

The first cousin of "I can't" is "I don't want to." Perhaps the inability to express your gratitude to your husband is one of the reasons you have a bitter attitude toward him and your marriage. Rebbetzin Jungreis says:

> People who cannot acknowledge kindness always find something or someone to criticize. They make miserable marriage partners, tyrannical parents, and selfish friends. They are convinced that everything is coming to them, that they are entitled to all the goodies in life simply because they are alive. No matter how much they are indulged, they are never satisfied. They just keep taking without feeling a need to give back.[3]

The Jewish sages define a *rich person* as the man or woman who is content with what they have. We as women must learn to take inventory of our possessions. We must learn to be thankful for all of them. This includes our spouses. Be grateful to the Lord for the husband He has given you, and be thankful and respectful to your husband who desires to be needed and wanted.

One of the greatest services a woman can perform for her husband is to respect him in thought, in word, and in action. All three are necessary, because they are interrelated. "Nevertheless let each one of you in particular so love his own wife as himself, and let the wife see that she respects her husband" (Eph. 5:33).

What you think affects what you say, and what you say affects how you act. No matter what shortcomings your husband may have, no matter how many changes he needs to make, always speak and act in a respectful way. The way you speak of him and act around him influences the way your children will perceive their father. It also influences the way other men and women think and behave toward your husband. Most importantly, it will deeply influence the disposition of your heart toward your husband.

> **HE SAYS...**
> **Love is not what you feel. Love is what you do.** *Works...not* **words...are proof of your love.**

A portion of the gift of life that a woman is privileged to give to her husband is her encouragement and support. Your husband needs someone who believes in him. He does not need someone who believes he is perfect. He needs someone who knows him intimately—his good points and his failings—and who still believes in him.[4]

I encourage you to put respect into action. Don't just agree that you *should* show respect. *Actually begin to act and speak and think with respect toward your husband.* Showing gratitude and respect to your husband will help him feel important in your life. As a result he will strive to become the man God wants him to be.

HOW TO AVOID THE DEATH OF YOUR MARRIAGE

What happens when you berate, disrespect, and take your husband for granted?

Psychologist John Gottman, PhD, has studied two thousand married couples, and he says that a minimum of five positive interactions for every negative interaction is essential to marital happiness. Dr. Gottman encourages plenty of touching, complimenting, smiling, and laughing, while warning against criticism, contempt, and defensiveness.[5] Some wives have a lot of "making up" to do.

Rebbetzin Jungreis states that there are fourteen positive commandments and seventeen negative commandments in Judaism concerned with speech. She goes on to say:

> God did not give us laws that are beyond our reach. Even our psychological makeup is designed to guard our tongues. Just consider— every organ in our body is either external or internal; for example, the eyes and nose are external; the heart and kidneys are internal. The tongue, however, is both internal and external and is protected by two gates—the mouth and the teeth, teaching us that before we use it, we must act with discretion, for the tongue is a most powerful instrument, and with it we can either kill or impart blessing.[6]

The Word of God says, "Death and life are in the power of the tongue, and those who love it will eat its fruit" (Prov. 18:21). When you berate your husband, you initiate the death of your marriage.

More than six million Jewish people died as a result of the evil reign of Adolf Hitler. However, Hitler did not murder these people with his own hands—he killed them with his tongue! He poisoned the German people to believe that Jews were subhuman creatures, and he convinced his killers that the Jews deserved to be eradicated from the earth. The power of life and death are in the tongue.

Remember this: what you don't say today can always be said tomorrow. But once you allow words to come out of your mouth, you cannot take them back. Scripture tells us that "out of the abundance of the heart the mouth speaks" (Matt. 12:34). Check the condition of your heart before you allow your mouth to speak. Ask yourself the question, "Am I honoring my husband with my speech, or am I tearing him down?" We can choose to uplift our husbands or to demean them with our speech.

If you have an argument with your husband, don't share that argument with your parents. It will be nearly impossible for them to forgive your husband for inflicting hurt on you, their daughter. It could take much longer than you desire for your husband to regain respect in the eyes of your parents.

Remember this rule of marriage: when your spouse offends you, God, in His infinite mercy, gives you a measure of grace to overcome the offense. However, when you share that offense with your parents, or others that love you, that same measure of grace is not afforded to them. Ultimately it will hinder them from the best relationship possible with your husband. Respect the private moments you have with your husband—good or bad—between just the two of you and the Lord. You will not regret it.

If you are a young woman who has not yet married the man of your dreams, take the time to carefully observe the man you are dating. How does he treat other people in his life? If you marry him, eventually this is the same way he will treat you.

My husband warns our young people about dating, "Be careful! Anyone can be good for four hours. But the real person is at home in a cage waiting to get out as soon as you say 'I do!'"

YOUR HUSBAND HAS GREAT VALUE

Your husband has true value in the eyes of God, just as you do. It is unfair to treat him as anything but royalty. Why are you surprised that he has lost that "loving feeling," if you spend hours demeaning him and pointing out his faults, constantly dwelling on his imperfections? You should live together in love.

Bob Moeller asks us to practice "cognitive dissonance," which occurs when our minds won't allow our feelings to exist contrary to our behavior.[7] When you feel that you have lost the feelings of love in your marriage, he suggests that for two or three days you treat your husband as if he is of enormous value to you.

> Go out of your way to show true respect, to listen with real intensity and without interrupting, and to compliment sincerely his strong traits. Keep your critical thoughts to yourself, and, instead, showcase his strengths to your friends and family. Anticipate his needs and put them first. If we treat someone with love, honor, and respect we are going to begin feeling it.[8]

Criticism causes men to become defensive, but admiration motivates and energizes them. A man expects and needs his wife to be his most enthusiastic fan. He draws confidence from her support and can usually achieve far more with her encouragement.[9]

It may be that you feel as though you do not know how to praise your husband. You may be thinking, *I only heard criticism when I was young. I never heard my parents praise each other. The only time they had long conversations with each other was when they argued.*

Sadly, I know far too many men and women who relate to this kind of thinking. However, today is the first day of the rest of your life! Ask the Lord today to break any generational curses over your life. Begin today to praise the Lord for His goodness. Begin to praise your husband and your children, and ultimately you will gain respect for them—and for yourself!

The Jewish *Mishna* is a commentary on the Torah, or the Word of God. In it, Jewish sages take the Word and interpret the wisdom within its pages to their congregants. One phrase found within the *Mishna* says this: "Who is mighty? He who masters control over himself." You too can become mighty. You can master what you say to yourself, to your husband, and to those you love. You can do this through the Lord's help in your life, for the Word tells us we can do all things through Christ who strengthens us (Phil. 4:13)!

Satan seduced Eve with his lying tongue and used it for evil. But you can allow the Holy Spirit of the living God to take your tongue, your thoughts, and your attitude and bring them under the control of His power, using your tongue and attitude for good. When you do, you will see great and mighty things come about as a result. You will have a husband who strives to develop to his fullest potential. Your children will be filled with confidence and hope for the future.

HINTS FOR HIM

I know you are probably tired of hearing that you are to love your wife as Christ loved the church, willing to die for her. But what can I say? This is the Word of the living God! You are to be obedient!

Every woman needs respect in order to function. Your wife will find it impossible to be the best wife she can be without your respect. Treat your wife as if she has value to you. She will then make sure she becomes invaluable to you. Accept her as she is, and soon she will want to improve anything about herself in order to bring you more pleasure.

Ask her opinion, and soon she will not make decisions until she makes sure you and she are in one accord. Let her know you understand how she feels, and soon she will strive to see the world through your eyes as well as her own. Let her know how proud you are of her, and soon she will see her full potential in Christ. Hug her often, for no reason other than the fact that you adore her, and soon she will be the woman who will make your home a sanctuary of joy and peace.

FROM DR. ANNE

Remember that you get what you give. This is never more true than in the area of giving and receiving respect. How you react to situations in your relationship will determine the extent that you will earn the consideration, courtesy, caring, and respect that you most desire. You will need to show him appreciation for his strength of character. Only God can develop this in you as you grow in spiritual obedience and maturity. Ask God to develop in you the ability to show the same measure of respect to your husband as you want him to show to you.

Respect is holding confidences. So many husbands have attempted to share their opinions, dreams, weaknesses, and vulnerabilities, only to have them disrespected by a loose-tongued wife who uses that knowledge as a weapon or to entertain her friends. He may take you into his confidence once...maybe he will be foolish enough to make another attempt...then he will close up, shut down, and the wall between you will be thick and high. He will have lost respect for you, and your weakness will be your loss!

Don't make what you believe to be the insensitivities of your husband your favorite topic of conversation with your friends. Instead, be willing to praise and support the authority God has placed over you. The words of your mouth are powerful and can impact the attributes, characteristics, and motivations of your husband.

If you recognize that this is a mistake you have made, God's grace and mercy are sufficient to build back a bridge of trust with your husband and to heal the wounds that may have resulted from your own insensitivity to his needs. When you come to God with a repentant heart, "He is faithful and just to forgive us our sins and to cleanse us from all unrighteousness" (1 John 1:9). Respect can be earned in direct proportion to the willingness with which you give it. With time, you will earn your husband's trust.

Don't ever forget that the role of nurturer and provider for you is not the only role your husband has to fulfill. Encourage your husband to be all that God wants and needs him to be. Be the supportive woman who will make it easier for your husband to hear and obey the voice of his Master.

Don't do anything to discount or sabotage your husband's efforts to do what God has asked of him. Be your husband's helpmate. Give him encouragement, not discouragement. Allow him to grow into the taller, larger role that God has for him.

Wait on the Lord. Renew your strength in Him. The man you have is the man God can use. Prayer will strengthen and develop the qualities that God wants—and that you want also. Prayer will perfect in him the respect and confidence he needs. When the woman of Proverbs 31:10 is diligent in the things that promote her family, her husband and children rise up and call her blessed, and her husband praises her. Isn't that the respect you really want? You can, just like Abraham, have all that you can see. The bottom line is prayer.

CLOSING PRAYERS

In this chapter, Dr. Anne and I have given you the tools to help you get out of the valley of despair. With God's help you can begin to experience a marriage filled with joy and expectation, one that will allow you and your husband to stand on mountains and view eternity.

PRAYER OF REPENTANCE

My Lord, forgive me for the foolish and hurtful things I have thought and said about my husband. I have not only hurt him, but I have disobeyed and disappointed You. I am so sorry. I have given approval to the disrespect of men and husbands by laughing at jokes that make them look weak and silly. My husband didn't deserve that. I also ask forgiveness for being discouraging and unsupportive when my husband has made an attempt to step out into the role You have ordained for him. I ask that You redeem the time that I have lost as an encourager while I have been looking at his faults and seeing my husband as inept and incapable. Please forgive me, Lord; I will change my ways and my confession.

PRAYER OF NEW BEGINNINGS

Dear God, You have truly blessed me by giving me the husband that I have. He is a good man, and the words of my mouth will say so! I will tell him often that I love him and appreciate him for all he means in my life. Help me to let him know how valuable he is to me. I will compliment him to others and refuse to partake in idle talk that is insulting to him or grievous to Your heart. I will stand up for my husband in the role You have for him to fulfill. Help me to be obedient to Your Word and the role You have created for me to fulfill. My God, guard my tongue from evil and my lips from speaking deceitfully. Without Your constant help and strength I can't do it. I know that You will renew my mind and help me uplift my husband with the love and respect I have for him. Amen.

FAMILY MAN

four

Train up a child in the way he should go,
And when he is old he will not depart from it.
—PROVERBS 22:6

RAISING A FAMILY takes hard work. Raising a family that loves the Lord takes a three-way partnership—you, your husband, and the Lord. Your children need the kind of father they can trust and the kind of father who trusts the Lord.

The Word of God instructs us to give honor to whom honor is due (Rom. 13:7). I would be remiss if I did not honor my husband for being a godly father. In this chapter it is my desire to *show* you the characteristics of a godly family man by allowing you to witness the interactions of my husband with his family.

I have seen this man weep at the birth of his children, spend hours with them while they needed training, smile with pride at their accomplishments, discipline them when discipline was earned, and fast and pray for them as we stood in the gap for their future. My children are blessed with a great father. I am richly blessed to have a husband who is devoted to his family.

From the moment we were married we wanted children, and God granted our desire. We have five beautiful children and, at the time of this writing, have four wonderful "in-loves" (otherwise know as "in-laws"). My husband and I feel that we now have nine children instead of five, and we are currently praying number ten into our fold. Our quiver is full.

47

I can truthfully say that every stage of their lives has been a joy to us. Even when trials come we can see the hand of God guide our children to the purposes He has for their lives. I give Him daily praise and thanks for the bountiful blessing He has so graciously bestowed on our family.

THE BIRTHS OF OUR CHILDREN

From the moment of conception for each child, we became a team in receiving and raising our children. Our roles have been different, yet as we combined our efforts and our prayers, parenthood has been a joy.

During my pregnancies, I remember my husband patting my belly every night as we prepared for bed. Lovingly, he called each child by name and said, "Though I haven't yet held you in my arms, I love you so much." He prayed a blessing over each child every night as we awaited their births. He wanted me to hold him close, putting my full body against his back so he could feel the kick of our precious children within my womb.

He often tells of the pride that he felt when he saw his firstborn, Tish, in the window of the nursery. He could hardly contain his joy as he watched this beautiful baby girl, full of life and hope.

Chris was very attached to his daddy and often wanted to be carried—even when he was no longer the baby of the family. No matter...Daddy carried him wherever he wanted to be carried, telling me, "He's not heavy—he's my little boy!"

Tina and I almost lost our lives at the time of her birth due to unexpected complications. I remember my husband's strong voice of support and his words of supplication as he laid hands on me and prayed the prayer of faith for a safe delivery for our baby and me. The morning after her delivery, he brought a yellow rose to present to his new baby daughter, saying, "I want to be the first man that gives flowers to this precious little girl."

When Matthew was born, the doctor asked if I wanted to hold him right after his birth. Glancing at my husband, I could see the look of awe on his face. "Will you please give our son to my husband first?" I asked the doctor. My husband reached for our son as if he was receiving a precious gift from God. As he welcomed Matthew to this world, Matthew's eyes opened, searching for the familiar voice he had heard so often while he was in his mother's womb. Once he placed his sight on this man who loved him so much, he smiled his first smile.

Our youngest daughter, Sandy, was born three weeks early, and she developed blood poisoning, which threatened her life. The first time we saw her after her birth, she was hooked up to every wire you could imagine. Tears ran down my husband's face as he put his massive hand in the incubation crib and placed it on her tiny chest as it struggled for breath. "Father, I ask that You breathe life into our baby girl and give her the fighting spirit to win this battle," he prayed. The Lord did exactly as my husband asked, and she still has that very same bold spirit to this day.

RAISING FIVE CHILDREN

I remember my "moments" of raising five children under twelve. They may have been trying moments at times, but they were never alone moments. My husband has always been there to partner with them and me.

When Tish was a Brownie in the Girl Scouts, she came home one day with one hundred boxes of cookies and announced she was going to win the badge for most cookies sold. "Great!" her daddy proclaimed.

"Daddy, you need to sell these boxes for me so I can get my badge!" Tish announced with equal conviction.

"Oh, great," my husband responded with a sigh. But he carried her door to door and sold cookies to friends, relatives, and church members until together they got their badge. The memory our daughter has of that experience is far greater than any badge; it is a precious gift to be treasured always.

Chris loved T-ball and was so excited to begin his new adventure. No matter how busy my husband's schedule became, he was at all the practices and all the games, ready to cheer Chris on. He spent hours in the back yard with Chris, helping him learn the game. As I prepared dinner in the kitchen, I could hear his encouraging words: "You can do it, son. You can do it!"

Through T-ball, Little League, Pop Warner, and varsity football...through elementary school, junior high, and high school, the ritual was always the same: "You can do it, son! You can do it!" Chris is no longer playing school sports, but to this day, when Chris is talking to his father about very important business decisions, I can hear my husband's careful instruction as he teaches his son all that he knows.

He continues to encourage Chris, "You can do it, son." He is so proud when his son teaches him things he doesn't know. He is never jealous, always proud.

Tina has always been the quiet one of the family, the tender one. She always did what was asked of her, yet always looked for her daddy's approval. I can still picture her running races in the backyard with her brothers and sisters, her long hair tied in a ponytail, flowing in the wind. She ran like a gazelle. "Look at me, Daddy! Look at me!" she called to her father as she ran.

Even when her voice was drowned by the clamor of the other children's voices vying for their father's attention, you could hear my husband's voice answer her with, "I see you, baby, and you are doing great! I am so proud of you! You're the fastest in the bunch!" As Tina heard his voice, she smiled that confident smile I now recognize in her own baby girl. She would run a little harder, never failing to keep an eye out for her daddy to make sure he was watching. He always was.

One Saturday night when our son Matt was nine years old, he asked to speak to his father after we had put him to bed. Thinking this was simply another ploy to stay up a little longer, I reminded Matt that his father had already prayed with him and was now studying his sermon for Sunday morning, a Saturday night ritual that he still follows.

"Mom, I need to talk to Dad. It's important." I noticed a very pensive look on his face as he lay on his folded arms looking toward the ceiling.

"Can I help you, Matt?" I asked him.

"No, Mamma. I need to talk to Daddy. This is very serious," he replied.

Worried, I thought, *What could it be?* I ran downstairs and interrupted my husband, who was deep in study. "Honey, Matt needs to talk to you! He tells me it is very important and can't wait for morning."

Seeing my concern, my husband left his study and began his walk up the stairs for the very important, mysterious meeting. I followed behind him, ready to enter Matthew's room. Turning to face me, he asked what, at the time, I felt was an unfair question: "Did Matt ask to see you as well?"

My response was quick, "No, but..."

He did not let me complete my sentence. "Then I will go into his room alone, and you can wait here." He gave me no choice but to have an attitude adjustment and wait at the foot of the stairs, praying that the Lord would give my husband wisdom for the *secret* Matt was about to share with him.

After what seemed to be hours, my husband came out of Matthew's room with tears in his eyes and a tender smile on his face. Comforted by the smile, yet concerned by the tears, I quickly asked him what had transpired.

"Matthew wanted me to pray a prayer of repentance with him, for he felt that he said things that offended the Holy Spirit today. He did not want to go to sleep with the offense on his heart," my husband told me, with tears freely flowing from his face.

I too joined in the tears. Mine were more for relief. Then I asked my husband this question: "Well, what did Matt say that offended the Holy Spirit?"

"I don't know. I didn't ask him," he replied.

"What? You didn't ask him! Why not?" I asked in disbelief.

"What is important is that we have taught our son to be sensitive to the Holy Spirit and to repent when he has done those things that have offended God. That, Diana, is the only thing that matters."

I was convicted. We held each other at the bottom of the stairs and had a good cry, thanking the Lord for the good things He had done and would do in our son's life.

One year, my husband and I were invited to speak in San Francisco at the International Full Gospel Business Men's Fellowship Conference, under the leadership of Demos Shakarian. Because of the nature of the invitation, my husband did not realize he accepted a date that would conflict with Sandy's tenth birthday. We had broken a huge rule: never be away for one of our children's birthdays! What to do?

My husband decided we would use his honorarium to pay for the children to come with us. We needed the funds to take care of other things and had to add more money to take care of their airfare, but we knew it was the only choice we had. There we were...the Hagee clan on the road to San Francisco.

Our schedule was hectic, as one can imagine.

One morning I was scheduled to speak at a women's prayer breakfast, and Daddy and Sandy had a date. Sandy knew this date was extra special. First, she was alone with her father. Second, her dad was scheduled to speak that evening before tens of thousands, and he was spending time with her instead of studying his sermon. This was very special. She walked tall as she left the room with her hand in the hand of the most important man in her life.

When my session was over, I went to our room to discover that Sandy and her father had not returned from their walk. It seems that Sandy, ever the most ambitious one, had asked the concierge for directions to a toy store near by. Wouldn't you know, our hotel was located just five blocks down from an FAO Schwarz store—the biggest toy store in the world? Sandy had hit the mother lode.

Several hours passed, and father and daughter returned to the room. By the look on both their faces, I could tell that Sandy had been triumphant, and Daddy had been... well... Daddy had been Daddy. "What did you get for your birthday, Sandy?" I asked, almost afraid to know.

With orchestrated pride, she stood in the middle of the room and boldly announced: "An elephant!"

"An elephant?" I asked as I turned to make careful eye contact with my husband. He looked up, and he looked down, but he never met with my glaring stare.

"Daddy said I could have one toy. Any toy I wanted." Part of her statement was our standard agreement with our kids: "Choose one." The second part, "any toy I wanted," was a new clause, one only Sandy could lobby for. As she ran to boldly announce to her brothers and sisters what she had received for her birthday, her father began to tell me what had occurred.

He had never been to an FAO Schwarz store. As he walked into this palace of toy wonder, he was amazed at the size of the store, the amount of toys to choose from, and, of course, the prices of the toys. But a promise was a promise. He let Sandy choose one toy, whichever one she wanted.

Sandy chose an elephant that was so big my husband could not carry it back to the hotel. So big that we would have had to buy an airline seat for it to come home with us. So big that he had to ship it home in a crate. So big that to this day I do not know how much it cost. He and Sandy share that secret, and I have convinced myself I am better off for not knowing.

> **HE SAYS...**
>
> **When you see your wife and loved ones at the end of the day, do you find ways to share joy and laughter? Or have you become so obsessed with work and toil that you have forgotten to develop the sound of laughter in your home?**

Our daughter is about to move into her new home with her husband, and she has a very special place for her elephant. There is only one thing that is bigger than that massive gray trophy, and that is the love and respect for the man who has never broken a promise—her daddy. A promise is a promise.

QUALITY TIME

A family man spends quality time with the whole family as well as with each child who has been given to him by God. Our meal times were, and still are, some of my most treasured moments in my life. We all gather around the table and share what the day has brought. My husband asks the children questions about their dreams, the answers of which usually conclude in waves of hysterical laughter.

When the children were young, we had few funds with which to do much. But it doesn't cost much to make precious memories. One weekend we would go to the movies, another weekend to the zoo, and then we would have a picnic the next weekend. Needing to purchase seven entrance tickets for the movie, we never had enough money left to buy the expensive goodies at the movie theater. So I did something I don't want you to tell anyone about! I packed my diaper bag with stuff. Not just any stuff. *Unique stuff.* I am of Hispanic descent, and I love to cook. I am a good cook. Every Saturday morning I make a Mexican breakfast for my family, a well-loved tradition.

When we had a "movie Saturday," I would pack breakfast tacos of beans and cheese, potato and eggs, and Mexican sausage. I wrapped them in foil and carefully packed them in my diaper bag, ready for our catered outing. We sat all five kids in front of us, sitting behind them so we could provide the matinee brunch. I waited for the theater to become dim before we made our move, so as to avoid the "movie Gestapo."

Once the theater was dark, you could see five little hands reach behind them one by one, whispering their desired choice of tacos, and the feast would begin. By the time you counted to ten, the people around us began to sniff out our secret as the aroma of fresh breakfast tacos competed with stale popcorn and shriveled hot dogs. Our children still remind us of the good times at the movies, and we laugh as we remember our little secret.

One year my husband announced that we were going to do something *big* with the children for our family vacation. *Wow,* I thought, knowing our budget could not afford much more than our standard trip to Grandma Hagee's and our annual visit to the battleship *Texas* at the San Jacinto monument in Houston. I called my dear friend Rachel, a travel agent, who understood our financial circumstances as she began her quest for the "big, yet cost-efficient" vacation.

Soon she called, with great excitement, to inform me that the Flag-ship Inn of Dallas, located across the street from Six Flags Amusement Park, had a family special: "Children under twelve *stay and eat for free!*" Eureka! God had provided for our "big" vacation!

We packed the kids in the station wagon and began our journey. We had perfected a ritual for staying at motels. My husband would cau-tiously drop me off at the front entrance to secure a room, asking for a crib for the baby. While I was doing that, he would drive our car to the back of the motel. In this way, management could not count the num-ber of heads in the car.

After I checked in, I reunited with my family, and we quietly made our way to our nonsmoking "double-double" home away from home. We all knew the regimen—Mom and Dad on one bed, the two girls on the other, the baby in the crib, and the two boys in sleeping bags on the floor.

We were much more considerate of restaurants. Due to the nature of our visits—usually laden with drink spills and an overabundance of cracker crumbs on the floor—we usually rotated our visits to favorite restaurants in order to spare the staff any added stress. I remember one Sunday night when my husband asked me if I wanted to go to a certain restaurant. "Oh, not there," I responded. "Not enough time has passed since our last visit!" We chose another restaurant to insure a good recep-tion when we arrived.

Ah, but this *big* vacation was different! We were out of town! We may never see these people again. We were relieved of any pressure. We were going to have fun on our first big vacation. When we woke up after our first night there, we went down to eat breakfast in the motel restaurant. We informed our kids that they could order anything off the menu that they felt they wanted to eat for breakfast. What a treat! These were not their normal choices. They were usually limited to the kid's menu.

Times were good. They were excited. Each day after breakfast we boarded the shuttle that took us into the amusement park and then back to the motel restaurant for lunch. Then it was back on the shuttle to the park, and back to the restaurant for dinner.

Finally, on the third day the manager came to our table. We knew this was too good to last. "Sir, I would like the ages of your children, please," our suspicious host said to my husband. Instantly my husband whistled his trademark alert to the kids, who leaped from their seats immediately and lined up in birth order.

"Give the man your name and age!" was my husband's command.

"Tish . . . I am eleven."

"I'm Chris, and I am eight."

"Tina . . . I'm four."

"My name is Matt. I'm this many," he said, holding up one hand with one finger and the second hand with two fingers.

The manager spared our one-year-old from the interrogation as he slowly nodded his head from side to side and walked away in disbelief. My husband ordered the kids back to their chairs and to their "big people's menu." It was a great vacation.

Lest you think I am married to the perfect family man, let me inform you that he doesn't do shots. When we took our children to the doctor for their vaccinations, he refused to hold them as they received their injections. Only when the traumatic ordeal was over would he then take them from me and hold them tight as he comforted them and assured his babies that they would be all right. It took me a while to forgive him of that, for my children associated me with trauma and pain and him with security and soothing comfort for most of their formative years.

A VALUABLE COMMODITY

I believe time to be our most valuable commodity. You and your husband must discipline yourselves to give your children as much of your time as possible, even when it is not convenient. From the time our children were young, we told them often that they would never be an inconvenience to us. If they needed a ride to and from an event, we were the ride. If they needed a place for their friends to gather, our home was that place. If they needed us to attend an event in which they were participating, one or both of us would attend that event. My husband says, "The reason God gave a child two parents is because between the two of them they make one good parent." A child should never feel that he or she is an inconvenience to your life.

As I am trying to meet the deadline of this book, our youngest daughter, Sandy, is beginning law school. The night before her first day she asked me if I remembered what I had done on the first day she attended kindergarten.

"Yes, I followed your bus to school!" I answered, as I recalled that vivid memory. Satisfied that I remembered, she smiled, and with that her father and I prayed a prayer of blessing over her first day at law school.

The next morning as my husband was leaving for the church office he asked if I was going to work on my book. Even though I knew the importance of the deadlines, I answered with what the Lord had confirmed to me would be my day's assignment. "Today I am going to law school." My husband smiled. He knew that what I was about to do was the right thing for Sandy's next big endeavor in life.

I waited for her orientation classes to begin, and then began my journey to another precious memory. I went to her first session. The staff allowed me into her class filled with three hundred students. Sandy was astonished as she spotted her mother proudly waving to her from the back corner of the room. She placed her hands on her hips and mouthed the word, "Why?"

I motioned back and mouthed, "Because I love you!" Even though she knew the answer, she smiled to confirm it once more. I waited in the car for her lunch break. While I waited, I called her new husband to see if he would like to surprise Sandy with a picnic lunch. Excitedly he agreed, and we wrote another wonderful chapter in the life of a very important person in our lives.

HE SAYS . . .

Your marriage must learn to endure adversity to reach achievement. Your attitude toward adversity will determine your accomplishments.

LOVE IN THE TOUGH TIMES

You might think that all our times with our children have been beautiful and without trouble, but that is not the case. Many tears have been shed, many meals have been fasted, and many prayers have been prayed on behalf of their lives. We have grieved together as Satan has tried in every one of our children's lives to bait them toward the wrong path. As the mother and father of five children, we have learned this great truth: a parent is only as happy as their saddest child.

Even though my husband has always shown a great amount of love to our children, he has also been their primary disciplinarian. My children filled many of my days with elaborate forms of animated discussions and negotiations as they pleaded, begged, and bargained with me not to tell their father of the wrong they had committed that day.

Not only did they fear his form of punishment—either a spanking or a restriction of some kind—but also they did not want to disappoint the man who loved them so much. I remember the wails coming from the garage where the chastisement would occur, which were followed by silence. When I entered into the room, I witnessed my husband holding our children and explaining why they should never again do what they had just been punished for.

Whether or not that offense he rebuked would be repeated depended on the child who had committed the action. Within our *quiver* you can find a combination of quick learners and strong-willed offspring. However, no matter what the response was to the punishment, one thing they all agreed upon was the fact that although their daddy loved them, he would not tolerate bad behavior or rebellion.

ESTABLISH SOME IMPORTANT "PARENT RULES"

You and your husband have to partner together in order to make a good family. One of the areas needing your partnership efforts is in the area of family relationships. You may find these "parent rules" that my husband and I followed to be of value to you in your own family.

1. Partner with your husband; don't compete for his leadership over your children.

One Saturday evening when Sandy was about six years of age, she came to me asking if she could do something. I explained to her why she couldn't, and she left the kitchen disappointed. About fifteen minutes later, she came back to me and proudly announced that her father had given her permission to do what I had already said no to.

Confused and upset, I asked her to follow me to her father's study where he was preparing for Sunday. As I have mentioned earlier, studying for Sunday is my husband's ritual to this day. My children learned early in life that Daddy easily agreed to anything on Saturday evenings.

HE SAYS...

**Submission does
not make a man
the "Hitler" of the
house. Submission
means that
he is a loving,
compassionate
leader who loves
his wife as Christ
loved the church.**

We walked into Daddy's study, and I asked if he had known that I had told Sandy *no* to the very same thing to which he had said *yes*.

"Sandy," he asked firmly as he realized what she had so cleverly maneuvered, "did your mother already say no to you?"

"Yes," she responded firmly.

"You know you are not supposed to come to me with something your mother has already said no to," he admonished.

"Yes, I do, but I have one question for this family!" Then, with her hands on her hips, my future lawyer asked this question passionately, "Who is running this house anyway?" Our children knew the answer to that question. *We both were.* Together, with the Lord's help and guidance, we would make the decisions that would train our children in the way they should go.

2. Set goals for your family, and stay focused on them. Do your best to help your children accomplish their goals.

Recently, my husband and I celebrated reaching one of the major goals we had set for our children and ourselves years earlier. We determined that each of our children should have a college education. As we watched our youngest child graduate from college, we gave thanks to the Lord for providing the resources to enable us to provide a college education for all of our children. Not only had God provided the resources, but He had also given our children the willpower and tenacity to accomplish this very valuable goal we set before them.

We gave them no option. A college degree was a must. Some of them got the revelation of the importance of being educationally prepared for life sooner than others, but eventually they all saw the light. When your children waiver on decisions that should be followed through to the end goal, stand firm with your spouse and be their strength as they are tempted to take the easy way out.

3. Pray daily with your husband for your children.

I know this is often a hard task to accomplish, because some men find it difficult to pray with their wives. I ask that you make it a point at the proper time of the day or night to ask your husband to pray with you on behalf of your children. I know that he will seldom refuse you if you do it in the right spirit. If he does refuse to pray with you, it will not be long before the Lord will convince him of the importance of the power available when two agree in prayer.

4. Bless your children and your husband daily.

When my husband leaves our home, I pray a prayer of blessing over him. He not only needs the prayer, but he also needs the encouragement that comes as the person he loves and partners with is putting a covering of blessing over his life. Make this your practice also. Then, together, bless your children. I never let my children leave on a trip without praying a prayer of blessing and protection over them. I believe God is waiting for you and your husband to release these prayers over your children. If not you, then who?

5. Pray for your children's spouses early in their lives.

I had such a long list of dos and don'ts for my children's spouses that the prayer was too long to pray, and it concentrated more on traits than the person. God helped me to shorten my prayer to be very powerful and effective. I learned to pray: "Father, my child's spouse is living somewhere in this world. Keep [him or her] safe and pure before You as You lead [him or her] into my child's life. Bring my child the person who will love [him or her] second to Christ. May they serve You together for the rest of their lives."

Some of you reading this book may be thinking that your children are now out of your home and that it is too late for you to learn some of these truths regarding your family. First of all, know and believe that it is never too late to begin to pray for and bless your children. Begin today.

Second, don't forget your grandchildren. Even though you don't have as much influence over them as their parents do, you still have a powerful impact on their lives. Rebbetzin Jungreis applies King Solomon's scripture, "A threefold cord is not quickly broken" (Eccles. 4:12), to a family composed of three generations. Rebbetzin stresses the importance of children hearing their grandparent's stories, basking in their love, and benefiting from their wisdom as precious, nurturing experiences that cannot be duplicated.[1] Even the grave cannot sever grandparent and grandchild relationships, which are based on unconditional love.

My paternal grandmother was someone who showed unconditional love to me. She died when I was only fifteen years old, but my memories of her and her undying love are still vivid and very much invaluable to me at fifty-two years of age. I remember her warm smile and tight hugs. I remember the many sacrifices she made for her grandchildren, whom she adored. I remember the times we spent in her home. She had no air conditioning in her home, and the sweltering heat of the Texas summer nights would take its toll on us. I remember waking in the middle of the night to find her standing over us waving a small hand fan until she made sure we were as comfortable as possible.

In the month of March of my fifteenth year, she gave me a beautiful gold ring with a single pearl surrounded by eight small diamonds. As she placed it on my finger, she said the gift symbolized her love for me. She died in October of that same year. Long after she was in heaven, I would look at that ring and remember the love she had for me, love even death could not diminish.

Instinctively I knew the value of that ring she presented to me. She was not a naturalized citizen and worked in a clothing factory as a seamstress. Early every morning she would dress in her best and walk to the bus stop, which would carry her to her long, tedious day. She saved money for years to present this special gift to her oldest granddaughter. It is one of the most treasured things I own, and it will forever symbolize her unconditional love for me.

I want to be that kind of grandmother. One who will love her grandchildren as the precious gifts from heaven they are. One who will encourage them to be all they can be in their Creator. One who will show them the love of Christ whenever they walk into the door of our home.

HINTS FOR HIM

Deuteronomy 32:7 tells us to "remember the days of old, consider the years of many generations. Ask your father, and he will show you; your elders, and they will tell you."

As a father you should remember the days past that gave you the most pleasure as a child. There may have been many things your parents could not give you financially, but they gave you plenty of time and love. Give that legacy to your children in handfuls.

If your parents did not give you these two invaluable gifts, then don't hesitate to break away from the heartaches of the past and begin new traditions of love and affection with your family. This decision is one you will have to make with God's help, but when you do, you will break generational curses that have kept your family from the blessings He has ordained for you.

Show your children the way they should go. If you demand honesty from them, then show them what an honest man looks like and talks like. If you demand respect from your children, then show respect to others around you, and they will follow in your footsteps. If you want them to have strong marriages, show love for their mother in their presence, which is the greatest training you can give them. If you want them to honor the Lord in their living and in their giving because you know it will bless their lives, then take them to the house of the Lord and let them see you give unto the Lord one-tenth of the resources He has provided for you.

There is a story of a young child who is climbing a mountain with his father. His father warned him to be careful as he climbed behind him. The son answered back, "Don't worry, Dad. I am putting my feet right where you put yours. I will be fine." The path you show your children is the path they will take.

If you are a grandparent, then tell your grandchildren of the love you have for them—and tell them often. Allow that love and the stories you tell them to be part of the legacy you leave them. The Talmud says, "He who loves his wife as himself and honors her more than himself, who guides his sons and daughters in the straight path...of him it is said, you shall know that your home is at peace."

FROM DR. ANNE

If we as women really want a man who is a "family man," we must be a part of establishing the environment that will allow the bonding that is a major part of the family. Only when home is placed in a priority position will each family member want to be present in that home. If there is chaos and friction, your husband will find reasons to work late, play more sports, or otherwise stay away. You really can't blame him. You would probably escape too if you had the chance.

Home must be a place that meets the needs of the family. Home must be a place of peace, security, respect, and harmony. What is needed to make this happen? There are some key issues that need to be addressed in most homes.

Christian lady, is your home a *home* or a *house*? Does your family come home only long enough to change clothes and sleep? When your husband wants to be with his family, what does he have to do to round up the lot of you so he can see all of you at one time? When you are all together, is this a time of joy or a time when problems are being solved? Do your children argue and compete for attention over the roar of the TV? Does everyone watch the clock so they can go about their own separate ways? Is the television actually the sound track of your lives?

If the last few sentences describe your family life, it is time to establish some important priorities. Encourage and reinforce family values, and, if necessary, retrain your family to make home their hub, oasis, and sanctuary. Home needs to be the place where each member is valued and loved. When home and family are comforting and pleasant, each member wants to be there.

Begin by *turning off the TV*! Once you have gone through the pain of separation anxiety, life will be more enjoyable. Be aware that the addiction tendency to media outlets will always be a temptation. *Just say no!* You will be amazed to find that the family is more content with what they have when not subjected to the hard-sell media marketing. Home will become the blessing God intends it to be.

Second, when your husband returns home each evening, make three positive statements to him before you unload the trials and tribulations of your day. First statement: "Hi, honey," "Hello, sweetheart," "Welcome home," or another loving greeting. Second statement: "I am glad you are safely home," "I have missed you," "I hope you had a good day," or "I love you!"

For your third statement, find at least one positive thing that has occurred during your day. If you think hard enough, you can come up with something! How about: "Little Sarah didn't shave *all* of the cat before your razor became dull," "Only *half* of the paper roll was flushed down the toilet before it stopped up," or "Junior's grades weren't the lowest in the class."

Your husband may wonder who the new you is and question what you did with his wife, but you can be certain he will be glad for the change. You will have the desires of your heart—a family man who enjoys being in the home he shares with the wife and children God has given him.

CLOSING PRAYERS

It was my desire in this chapter to show you the characteristics of a godly family man by letting you sneak into our family life and observe my own husband's demonstrations of love and support to his children. In the Bible are many examples of godly fathers. One example comes from the apostle Paul, who filled the role of *spiritual father* for many first-century Christians. In 1 Corinthians 11:1 he says that he learned from Christ Himself. We can find no better example of how to be a loving parent than by following the example of Christ. In 1 Thessalonians 2:11–12, Paul says this: "For you know that we dealt with each of you as a father deals with his own children, encouraging, comforting and urging you to live lives worthy of God, who calls you into his kingdom and glory" (NIV). Ask God to help you deal this way with your children—whether you are a mother or a father.

PRAYER OF REPENTANCE

Father God, forgive me for not using Your guidelines when preparing my home for my husband and my children. As my heavenly Father, You always have time for me, and You hear my cry when I am in need. I have not always given of myself to my husband and my children as I should have. I have allowed my time to be stolen by the demands and expectations of others. I have busied my life with trivial matters that will make no eternal difference.

I haven't encouraged our children to set the expectation that home is where the best quality time is spent. I have let the model for my family be set by the world and not by Your Word. I have let the expectations You have set before my husband, my children, and me to be lowered. I repent and will change my ways.

I will direct the atmosphere of our home to be nurturing and caring for my husband and children. I acknowledge that I have not consistently helped to create the atmosphere that will enable my husband to be a godly family man. I ask that You forgive me for the times I have usurped his authority with our children. Forgive me for not showing honor or respect toward my husband before my family. I will ask forgiveness from my husband and my children, and I will do all that I can with Your help to create a peaceful and joyful and godly home.

As a single woman, forgive me for dating men that I know are not family men. I cannot change them; only You can. I will look and wait on the man that I know will honor You and Your Word and will be a godly father to the children You will give us. Amen.

PRAYER FOR NEW BEGINNINGS

Precious Jesus, I acknowledge Your generosity and Your blessings to my family. Father God, You established the family and hold it to a high standard. Thank You for the opportunity to guide and influence my family in obedience to Your ways and Your Word. Our home will be a place You will be proud of, a place of peace, comfort, and love. You will know that You are welcome in my home at all times.

My husband will be proud of our home and will love to be there. My husband will enjoy my company, and I will prefer his company to any other friend. I will pray a blessing over my husband and children every day. I will partner with him to be the parents You have destined us to be. Together we will lead our children in the way they should go.

Your ways are the highest ways. Love, restoration, mercy, and grace will be the words over the entrance to our home, and all who enter will know that You are placed in highest regard. Your presence will be honored in our home always. Amen.

PROVIDER

> If anyone does not provide for his relatives, and especially for his immediate family, he has denied the faith and is worse than an unbeliever.
>
> —1 TIMOTHY 5:8, NIV

> Her husband has full confidence in her and lacks nothing of value. She brings him good, not harm, all the days of her life.
>
> —PROVERBS 31:11–12, NIV

SECULAR HUMANISM IS the world's universal religion, and, like all other religions, it has commandments. Commandment number one is, "Take care of *yourself*, or no one else will." When self-centeredness takes front seat, it isn't long before the world becomes a small place—with each person concerned only for those things that encompass his or her own surroundings.

A self-centered way of life is birthed out of immaturity. Self-centered people are like very small children who are preoccupied with only their own needs and wants. The "me first" mentality is contrary to the principles of Christianity. True maturity can only develop when our lives revolve around *others* rather than ourselves. Maturity means growing in awareness of others and the world around us. A decreased concern for your own needs and an increased concern for the well-being of others demonstrate complete human and spiritual maturity.

Unfortunately, sometimes our development in maturity grinds to a halt at midstream. Some people become adults without experiencing a complete transition from a *me-centered* life to an *others-centered* life.

GROW UP FIRST; THEN MARRY

Marriage is for grown-ups. Maturity is a requirement that is often over-looked when choosing a mate. Developmental disturbances, coupled with the me-first mentality of humanistic theology, are destined to bring grief and trouble to any marriage. A man who is not fully mature in this area of his life is not ready for the commitment and the responsibility of marriage. However, a *Christ-centered* man is able to serve his spouse and children unselfishly.[1]

During my college years, a college friend of mine dated a very good-looking college jock for a while. They really made an attractive couple. With her stunning brown eyes and adoring smile, she was beautiful, and his muscular physique and great looks complemented her beauty. All seemed perfect.

However, it soon became evident that he was "too good to be true!" He was always "short on cash," and what little he did manage to get from his affluent family was quickly squandered on "his needs." Most of their dates were Dutch, and my friend often had to cover the whole night's expenses because he was, once again, "short on cash." "I'll make it up later," he always promised. But he did look great in a pair of Wranglers!

My friend would be quick to tell you that her priorities were not quite right when choosing who to date at that point in her life. Remember this ever-simple rule: *you will eventually marry someone you date.* Duh! This may sound a little too obvious, yet you have no idea how many young women tell me, "We're only dating!" when, as their pastor's wife, I question their choice in men. They have a requirement list for their future husband, but none for the men they date.

What does "only dating" mean? It usually means, "I'm only going out with this person because he can fill my weekend." Yet repeatedly these "fill-in" individuals end up filling a woman's lifetime with sadness and strife.

The young man who was dating my friend not only did not provide for her financially during their courting experience, but he did not provide for her emotional needs either. The self-centered person is too preoccupied with his or her own needs and is blind to the needs of others.

Immaturity will always consume more than it will produce—both financially and emotionally. The immature man will take this same philosophy into the marriage relationship, creating a weak foundation that will soon crumble under the pressures of life.

Later in my college friend's life, the Lord brought to her the man He had chosen for her from the beginning of time. Dan had worked his way through college and was working his way through medical school when they met. Their first date was dinner at a local restaurant and a night at the symphony. My friend felt like a queen—as it should be.

Their relationship blossomed and soon led to the marriage altar. At that stage of her life, my friend was not yet looking for financial security in a relationship; what she needed was someone to complement her whole person—spiritually, emotionally, physically, and financially. In fact, after they married she became their sole financial support while her husband completed his residency in obstetrics. She was glad to fill that role because her husband was supplying her emotional, physical, and spiritual needs. They were a team.

> **HE SAYS . . .**
>
> I asked a beautiful young lady just out of college, "What kind of man would you like to marry?" She joyously responded, "I want a husband who can dance, looks good, and likes what I feed him." "That's great," I responded. "You've just described Trigger."

Dan has been a great husband and father to my friend and their children. He has provided for them in so many ways, and he is teaching his own children how to provide for their own.

GOD SAYS, "PROVIDE FOR YOUR FAMILY"

The Word of God is very clear on its position for a man who can—but won't—provide for his family. It says, "He has abandoned the faith!" (See 1 Timothy 5:8.) My friend, this is a very serious charge. Our faith is the foundational cornerstone of our being. It is the source of our relationship with our Savior. To be accused by the counsel of God for "abandoning the faith" is far more serious than I can fathom. In this Scripture verse, the Lord continues by describing such a man as "worse than an unbeliever." Why? Because an unbeliever does not know the Word of God or what God expects of him; therefore, he has not abandoned it.

It is not possible to *abandon* something unless you once possessed that thing. Therefore, the man who "abandons the faith" is a man who knows what God expects of Him, yet he *refuses to do those things,* turning his face away from the will of God for his life. According to God, that man is worse than the man who never believed.

Dr. Harley is clear in his statements regarding the research he did about men and women in the area of financial needs. He states that a woman may not marry a man totally for his money, but money certainly has something to do with her choice of the man she decides to marry. Most women not only expect their husbands to work, but they also expect them to earn enough money to take care of their families.[2]

I come from a family with a very strong work ethic. Both my grandmothers worked very hard inside and outside of the home. One, as I mentioned earlier, worked as a seamstress, and the other worked as a maid until she was over seventy years of age.

My father was a truck driver, transporting produce throughout America, when I was born. Later he worked double shifts as a civil service worker in the field of computers. Eventually he owned a very successful produce company and then a restaurant. Recently, he interviewed for—and accepted—a new job at the age of seventy-one!

By the age of thirteen, my mother was working as a waitress to help her family financially and to put herself through private school. She married my father and raised a family at home. She worked by his side in the produce business and in the restaurant they later owned. She is now seventy-two years of age and serves at John Hagee Ministries in the shipping department, working circles around young men one-third her age. She faithfully prays over every package that leaves our ministry.

My father-in-law worked all the days of his life. He worked as a Merchant Marine for Standard Oil during the depression. He served the Lord in the ministry for fifty-three years as a pastor and evangelist. After retiring, he and my mother-in-law managed the mobile home park they built twenty years earlier in anticipation of their retirement. He managed and maintained that park until his passing at seventy-eight years of age.

My mother-in-law began to care for a household of brothers and sisters at the age of nine, and she worked her way through seminary by teaching in the very same school from which she eventually graduated. She worked tirelessly by her husband's side for fifty-three years. During those years she held many positions, serving at times as head of the women's ministry, children's church director, Christmas and Easter pageant director, costume designer and maker, organist, and Sunday school teacher. She was a singer and accordion player with her husband and sons during their time in evangelism, as well as being one of the best prayer warriors I have ever had the privilege of knowing. She did all of this while caring for her husband and four boys. After retiring from the ministry, she worked as a cafeteria worker at a local school until she was seventy-five, and just recently, at the age of ninety-one, she turned her management responsibilities for the mobile home park over to her son Jack. She is still a consultant—on full salary, I might add.

My husband works fourteen to sixteen hours a day, and he has done so since he was twelve years of age. His motto: "You can put in a half day's work; I don't care which twelve hours you choose." He has taught our children this same work ethic—a legacy they will leave to their own children.

My family has always accepted work as a necessary part of life and is thankful for the opportunity to put in a full day's labor. Therefore I find it difficult to identify with the man who refuses to work and provide for his family.

I often hear unemployed men say, "I'm waiting for the right job," or "I was trained in a certain field and am waiting for an opportunity in that field." Don't wait—yield. Yield to what the Lord has set before you. Sometimes the hardest decisions you must make require humility and obedience before provision comes. Learn to yield to the voice of God.

> Be anxious for nothing, but in everything by prayer and supplication, with thanksgiving, let your requests be made known to God.
> —PHILIPPIANS 4:6

There is no alternative for work. The Creator's position is very clear: Don't abandon the faith! Provide for and protect your family.

THE IMPORTANCE OF GOD'S TITHE

I must take the subject of financial provision one step further to *tithing*. I minister to many wives who are tormented by the fact their husbands refuse to give back to the Lord one-tenth of what the Provider has allowed them to earn. A man who rejects the principle of tithing cannot understand the feelings of a woman who believes and trusts in the Word of God regarding prosperity.

She knows that the Lord requires the tithe. She knows that He will provide blessings to those who obey the Lord with their tithe. She knows that the Lord promises to devour the enemies of her family when her family is obedient in the tithe. She knows that when her family brings its tithe into the storehouse of the Lord, He will not allow the fruits of the family member's labor to be destroyed. She knows.

Yet her husband refuses to tithe. When a woman at Cornerstone Church asks me what her alternatives are when she finds herself in this situation, I must tell her that, based on the Word of God, she does not have many options. She must be obedient to her husband's decision. If she is a godly woman of the Word, she knows what the Word teaches will be the outcome of her husband's choice. This knowledge can be tormenting to her.

If you find yourself in the position of being married to a man who will not give the Lord His tithe, you must wait on the Lord to convince your husband of his need to be obedient to God's Word. Wait for your husband to reject the darkness of his choice and embrace the light, yielding fully to the things of God. This is a very difficult position to be in, and hundreds of thousands of believing families are not blessed to their full potential due to their lack of obedience in the tithe.

This is a question that must be settled before the marriage takes place. Find out exactly what your future husband's plans are for the financial security of you and your family. Make sure his plan is a realistic one and that it is in compliance with the Word of God.

Ask him what his position is on the tithe. If you are married, and your husband refuses to tithe, then you must obey his wishes, pray, and wait. Don't argue about your husband's lack of obedience. You, as a wife, must also learn to yield to the Holy Spirit and wait on His time.

WHAT ABOUT THE WOMAN WHO SPENDS TOO MUCH?

Now, what about the woman who has a husband who works hard for his family but can never fully provide for their needs because of the wife's careless spending habits? What does God's Word say about this woman?

Jokes are often made of men and women in this situation. Have you heard the one about men who have pierced ears? They seem to be better equipped for marriage; they've already experienced pain and are used to buying jewelry.[3]

Part of what contributes to the debt problem in America is our demand for *instant gratification*. We live in a society where instant gratification takes too long. A man and a woman marry, and they instantly want what their parents have taken a lifetime to assemble. This couple never saw the apple crates their parents used for chairs or the mismatched, hand-me-down furniture. *Generation X* is only perpetuating what the *Baby Boomers* began, which is trying to duplicate what the *Greatest Generation* took years to put together.

The Greatest Generation survived the Depression, and they did so debt free. The next generation invented the word *debt*. Debt is now so common to twelve-year-olds that they carry credit cards instead of cash. A twelve-year-old, however, doesn't pay the bill at the end of the month. The two most frequent causes for divorce are *sexual dysfunction* and *financial problems*. Both of these problems are rooted in something deeper than the way in which they are manifested.

As a woman, you will be held accountable for how you help your husband maintain financial order within your marriage. Your husband should be able to have *full confidence* in you and should "lack nothing of value" because of your management of the household budget. (See Proverbs 31:11–12.)

> **HE SAYS . . .**
>
> **Don't let your marriage be destroyed by your inability to control your financial spending.**

Many women who manage the checkbook at home fail to keep precise records, allowing the account to be in such disarray that they don't know where they stand financially. With their out-of-control spending habits, they refuse to let the balance in their checking account determine what they will spend. Instead, they charge up to the maximum limit on their credit cards, stressing their budget and creating debt. Satan has them trapped.

What to do? Stop! Stop now! Repent! Acknowledge that you have done wrong, and make up your mind that, with the help of the Lord, you will establish a spending plan that will help you and your family get out of debt—and stay out!

A spending plan is a "necessary good." If you are a woman who is tempted often to buy more than your income can afford, a spending plan can help you set priorities for a quality of life you can truly enjoy.

During my college days, I had a very special friend who was from the south. She was one of a long line of *steel magnolias*. She met and married a very conservative young man from England. Oh, what a pair they made. One day after they had moved away from our city and back to my girlfriend's southern hometown, she called me, rather frustrated. "I'm so mad at my husband," she told me in her charming southern drawl, which had dramatically increased since she moved back home. "He is not playing fair!"

"What do you mean?" I asked her.

She explained to me that she had asked her husband to purchase a kitchen gadget for her that was outside their budget. Instead of acknowledging the request to be out of their spending plan, he put the ball in her court and asked her this question: "How dear is it to you?"

To say the least, this was an unfair question. My friend realized that her desire for that gadget had little value when put into a financial perspective. Regardless of her desire for that gadget, the point was settled . . . no purchase.

THE IMPORTANCE OF A BUDGET

Dr. Harley recommends three kinds of budgets—a *needs* budget, a *wants* budget, and an *affordable* budget.[4]

A *needs budget* should include the monthly costs of meeting the necessities of your family's life. It should include those things you and your family would be uncomfortable without.

The *wants* budget should include the cost of meeting all your needs *and* your desires. Your desires, or wants, are things that bring special pleasures to your life. These should be within reason, of course.

In order to make positive lifetime changes in your spending plan, it is important to be realistic. A *needs budget* begins when a man comes to his wife and requests that they put a budget together. "Let's start with the basic necessities—food, shelter, and clothing. Choose any two," he demands.

The *wants budget* is established when his wife responds by handing him her "Wants List." However, that wants list should not include weekly visits to the spa by chauffeured limousine.

Now we come to the *affordable budget*. This realistic list is established by subtracting the items on that *needs list* from the amount of income your family has. Then what is left can be applied for some of the items on your *wants list*. This will help you to define "how dear" your wants are to you. Eventually you will learn to determine how many wants you will be able to include in your budget, based on the money you have left after your needs have been met.[5]

Remember this rule: you will seldom find something as much fun to own as it is to *look forward to owning*.[6]

Life is more than wants. Don't make the mistake of always making your wants your goals. As want after want is attained, they will become your idols, and you will discover that the attainment of wants does not bring satisfaction. Satisfaction is still nowhere to be found. If you continue down this haphazard path, you will discover that the balance between financial provision and emotional, physical, and spiritual provision is nonexistent.

Husband and wife drift apart as they try to meet their own desires; the children receive the residual of their time and affection. The "self-gratification" parents take care of themselves first and hope their children will benefit.[7]

THE LORD PROVIDES THE BALANCE IN YOUR BUDGET

Support one another as you stay within the spending plan you and your husband agree on. Don't create any unnecessary stress or conflict for your marriage. Be satisfied with your spending plan, and set goals for your future that will help build a strong marriage and an example for your children to follow in their own lives.

Ask your husband to forgive you for the bad spending habits you have developed that have kept you and your family in debt. Ask him to agree with you in prayer that you will turn from spending, no longer using spending as a placebo to keep you from dealing with the real emotional issues that may be troubling you.

You may find that you need to turn over the control of the family budget to your husband, or at least come into mutual agreement before anything

> **HE SAYS...**
>
> **The less able you are to experience inner peace, the more you will require material symbols like a bigger house, faster car, bigger boat, or larger salary to satisfy your thirst for happiness.**

is spent outside your agreed-upon spending plan. It may be difficult in the beginning to surrender your control, but it will be much easier than picking up the pieces of a broken marriage.

Thank your husband often for providing for you and your family. It is difficult to go to a job day after day that may be full of conflict or where unbelievers surround him continually. Let him know often that you don't take his sacrifice lightly.

As he walks out of the door each morning, bless him with favor, wisdom, and discernment for his job. You will be amazed at what the spoken Word of God can do when proclaimed over your husband every day.

Support your husband in the tithe. Teach your children early about the importance of giving to God a portion of what He has so graciously allowed you to produce. Know that when you obey the Lord and hearken to His voice, He will cause His blessings to overtake you!

> "Bring all the tithes into the storehouse,
> That there may be food in My house,
> And try Me now in this,"
> Says the LORD of hosts,
> "If I will not open for you the windows of heaven
> And pour out for you such blessing
> That there will not be room enough to receive it."
> —MALACHI 3:10

This portion of Scripture is the only place in the Word of God where God asks His body to test Him.

When you give the Lord His portion, He will bless what you have left and cause it to multiply, bringing you provision beyond what you could ever think possible. Be ready for His blessings, because our God is faithful!

HINTS FOR HIM

You must accept the truth that there is no option but to provide for your family. If you have had a difficult transition from the "me-centered" life to the "others-centered" life, then take certain steps to correct your attitude.

1. *Identify the problem.* There is some self-concern in all of us. But if this concern has prevented you from providing for your wife physically, emotionally, spiritually, or financially, then it must be identified and addressed.

2. *Rely on the grace of God.* Your Creator will never reveal your sin to you, convict you of your sin, and then not provide a full measure of grace necessary for the change He *expects* of you.[8]

3. *Communicate.* Your spouse has been praying for change in your marriage, especially about the attitude you have regarding provision. Let her know that your lives will be different from now on, and that together you can make a positive difference in your relationship.

4. *Take action.* The Word of God tells us to "write the vision and make it plain" for all to understand (Hab. 2:2). It is important to follow through with the "provision plan" you put in place, using the Scriptures as your guide. The Lord is faithful, and He will show you how to provide for your wife and children spiritually, emotionally, physically, and financially. Be patient, and trust that your plan will be fulfilled with your dedication and God's help.

5. *Have compassion.* Your family has suffered for your lack of obedience to the Word of God. They have seen someone they love not blessed because of disobedience. Learn to put yourself in their place in order to understand the difficult journey they have walked with you. It will help your own road to recovery.

Provision comes in different forms. Even though financial provision is a very important form—physical, emotional, and spiritual provision are equally as important. The main essence of provision is to give to others what has been given to you by your Father in heaven—unconditional love.

Charles Spurgeon told the story, "Once, while riding in the country, I saw on a farmer's barn a weather vane on which was inscribed these words: 'God is love' I turned in at the gate and asked the farmer, 'What do you mean by that? Do you think God's love is changeable, that it veers about as the arrow turns in the wind?' The farmer said, 'Oh, no! I mean that whichever way the wind blows, God is still love.'"[9]

> Jesus answered and said to him, "If anyone loves Me, he will keep My word; and My Father will love him, and We will come to him and make Our home with him."
> —JOHN 14:23

FROM DR. ANNE

During my years of counseling, I have found that security, on all levels, is the thing that a woman needs most. She may mask that need in a number of ways, but security is the basic issue. God made us this way, and He provided for our needs to be met by defining the roles of men and women as He did in His Word.

It is important that you are able to make your husband feel needed. A man who doesn't feel needed is not going to provide. If you are so independent that you don't need your husband, is it any wonder that you are not happy? He probably wonders why you keep him around. If you don't show satisfaction and appreciation for the effort that is made for you, why should he try to satisfy you further?

There are three kinds of women who will never have the provider they may say that they want:

1. *The over-achieving woman who discounts her husband's ability to provide.* The wife who makes it clear that she doesn't need anything from her husband that she can't provide for herself will have a husband who provides little or nothing.

2. *The woman who clings too tightly, draining the energies from her husband.* The wife who holds so tightly to her husband's time that she doesn't want him to work and spend time away from her will get him fired very quickly.

3. *The woman who has so many whims and wants that her husband can't keep ahead of her expectations.* A wife whose

wants are never ending will frustrate her husband. Her wants are always ahead of his provision, so she uses a credit card. She is more interested in keeping a standard that is equal to her friends than the standard that she and her husband can afford. He is burdened under the mountain of debt and still has a dissatisfied wife. He will soon stop trying.

On the other hand, faith and trust in your husband's abilities to be the provider for your family will set the environment for him to gain the strength and self-confidence he requires.

The wife who is a good steward with what her husband earns is the Proverbs woman who is called **blessed** by her husband. A clean, neat appearance and home, a wife with a smiling face, clean, well-behaved children, and a car clear of debris give a husband encouragement. When a man's wife, children, home, and car all look "on their last leg," he starts the day with a failing attitude.

Learn to be creative in the ways you find to have your needs and wants—and those of your family—met. Bargains are everywhere! Garage sales and resale shops have been a blessing to all of us. Get excited over the designer dress or accessory you find in a resale shop for a mere fifty cents. The Holy Spirit will lead you to bargains.

God told men in His Word to provide protection (both emotionally and physically), food, shelter, clothing, spiritual comfort, and teaching. Men are to provide for their families those things that God has made available to everyone. Learn to be the appreciative, supportive helpmate God intended you to be to your husband.

CLOSING PRAYERS

There is a saying in Spanish that translates, "A cage even though it's made of gold is still a cage." Life is much more than possessions. When my husband performs the funeral service of a church member, the family members never comment on the amount of wealth their loved one made or left behind. These family members remember the time and love that were spent with their dearly departed loved one.

Stay within the balance of the Word of God. Your Provider promises to care for you. In turn, you must take care of your loved ones as you hear His voice and obey His commandments.

PRAYER OF REPENTANCE

Father, forgive me, for I have been wasteful with the resources You have given us. I have spent money unwisely; I have been materialistic and purchased things we didn't need with money we didn't have. I have failed to be a good steward of our blessings. I have not been appreciative of the efforts my husband has made to be the provider for our family. I have not participated in his success. I have hindered him in providing for our family and have not taught my children to spend wisely or to give of the tithe unto the storehouse of the Lord. I repent of my actions, and with Your help I will turn from my ways and walk the path You have chosen for me.

PRAYER OF NEW BEGINNINGS

Father God, I acknowledge You as my Provider. You are the source of every good and perfect gift that I receive. You meet all of my needs and the needs of my family. I will thank You for Your provision every day. I declare this day, in Jesus' name, that I will prepare a spending plan with my husband, and I pledge to follow that plan with joy and discipline. We will tithe to You one-tenth of what You have allowed us to produce. I will trust You to provide blessings that we will not be able to contain. I will communicate to my husband that I need him to provide for me emotionally, physically, and spiritually. I will pledge to him that I too will try to meet his needs, so together we can make our marriage a thing of satisfaction and joy. I will thank my husband and appreciate his sacrifice for my family and me as he leaves for work, and I will proclaim a blessing over him each day. Thank You, Lord, for the grace and strength You will provide to make all this possible. Amen.

Pray for us: for we trust we have a good conscience,
in all things willing to live honestly.
—HEBREWS 13:18, KJV

Having your conversation honest among the
Gentiles: that, whereas they speak against you as
evildoers, they may by your good works, which they
shall behold, glorify God in the day of visitation.
—1 PETER 2:12, KJV

TRUTH IS NARROW. What would you do if you were hiking and came to a wide river, and learned that there was only one bridge down the river a mile or two? Would you stomp in anger and complain about bad planning? Would you say that the bridge was too far away and should have been built right where you are standing? I doubt it! To the contrary, you would be thankful that there was a bridge, and you would gladly walk to it and use it to get to the other side.

If you went to the doctor and discovered that you needed a prescription for medication, wouldn't you want *both* the doctor and the pharmacist to get the dosage exactly right before you took the medication home, trusting that all was in order?

When you get on an airplane, do you have faith that the pilot will listen to the traffic control operators, who will in turn follow their instrument panels with complete accuracy as they guide the plane through the skies?

Truthfulness and honesty are absolutes in life, and they must never be compromised. Truth and honesty are like fine china. They can be broken. They can be mended. But they can never be the same again without the restoration of the Lord Jesus Christ.

79

There must be absolutes in life. In a world where men have redefined history, values, and goals, we must look to something and someone to be the same yesterday, today, and forever. We know that someone to be Jesus Christ. He never changes. He never fails. And we are to pattern ourselves after Him.

Honesty is defined as "a refusal to lie, cheat, or deceive in any way." An honest person shows fairness and sincerity. An honest person is genuine.

The Lord clearly speaks to us in the Book of Micah: "He has shown you, O man, what is good; and what does the LORD require of you but to do justly, to love mercy, and to walk humbly with your God?" (Micah 6:8).

Truth and honesty are essentials in life whether you are a man or a woman. One of the things that every woman needs from her marriage is a sense of security. Dr. Harley states, "Security is the bright golden thread woven through all of a woman's five basic needs (affection, conversation, honesty, financial support, family commitment). If a husband does not keep up honest and open communication with his wife, he undermines her trust and eventually destroys her security."[1]

HUSBANDS WHO LIE

It is crucially important for a woman to be able to fully trust the man she marries—before she marries him, every moment of every day, and for every day of her future. She must be able to trust the information her husband gives her about his past, present, and the future. Without trust, she cannot build a solid marriage foundation. If she cannot trust her husband, she will begin to feel isolated from him and will eventually grow further and further away from him, emotionally and physically.

Honesty must be a foundation stone in marriage. According to the survey we conducted, women desire honesty from their husbands above five other qualities that we have discussed in earlier chapters, including faithfulness, leadership, respect, his ability to be a godly family man, and his being a good provider.

However, some men struggle with honesty. Some husbands find it easy to lie to their wives, often about minor things. Others manipulate or control their wives by the lies that they tell. Some men would fit into the category of a "born liar."

This man has continually told lies about the smallest of things even from a young age. He may say he was working when he was really playing cards. He is easily caught in his lies by simple fact-finding, yet he will explain his lies away with jokes or pleading a "poor memory."

This man finds it very difficult to change, because he can't acknowledge he has a problem. He has never come to know the voice of his conscience. Even a child knows the importance of honesty.

A young woman was basking in the tropical sun as she lay on the sandy, white beach. A young boy came up to her carrying a sand bucket and beach towel. He stood awkwardly over her without a word until she acknowledged his presence. "Can I help you?" she asked curiously.

"Do you believe in God?" the little boy blared.

Surprised by his boldness, the woman quickly replied, "Yes."

His next question came quickly: "Do you go to church every Sunday?"

Again she answered, "Yes."

Then he asked, "Do you read your Bible and pray every day?"

Once again she answered, "Yes!"

She was now overtaken by curiosity as he asked his last question. "Great! Would you hold my quarter while I go swimming?"[2]

When a man refuses to acknowledge the importance of honesty in his life, he will make trust within a marriage almost impossible.

Sometimes a man will tell his wife lies because he believes it will keep him out of trouble. It becomes very easy for him to lie to his wife, and he expresses no remorse unless he is caught. Often, because of his lack of true repentance, he will fake remorse to make the offended party quickly "forgive and forget." Unlike the born liar, he usually resorts to lying when he is under pressure.

A young man got twenty-five dollars too much in his pay envelope and said nothing to his employer. As the week progressed, the employer realized his error and docked the young man's next paycheck.

When the young man noticed the shortage, he immediately went to his employer. "Excuse me, sir, but I am twenty-five dollars short this week," he said.

"You didn't complain last week," his boss replied.

Thinking quickly, the young man replied, "No, sir, I don't mind overlooking one mistake. But when it happens twice, then it's time to say something."[3]

When a problem with dishonesty is acknowledged, a man can, with the help of the Lord and his wife, learn to be honest in the marriage relationship. He can learn to avoid the stressful situations that set him up to fail in maintaining truthful communication with his loved ones.

Some men believe that there are some truths that are too hurtful for their wives to handle, so they tell lies to "protect her." This man is truly bothered by his lies. He considers lying a necessary evil, done to protect his wife and family. For example, he may be the person who takes care of the finances, and he needs to borrow money because he is not able to make ends meet. He has a plan to pay back the loan, so he tells his wife everything is fine financially to keep her from worrying.

He is lying to protect her. Even though it bothers him, he feels it is worth it. This creates a false sense of security in the relationship, and as soon as the lie is exposed (and it always will be), his world comes tumbling down around him. His lies will do irreparable damage to his marriage.[4]

It's possible that the widower in the following story would say that he was lying to "protect" the feelings of the woman he met. A widower was entertaining a woman with whom he had gone on a blind date that had been arranged by his matchmaking children. The homely old maid began to confess her feelings of insecurity to the widower, Mr. Thompson. "I am at a low ebb in my life," she told him. "I have no self-worth. I don't feel attractive."

In a very affirmative voice, the kind gentleman replied, "Let me assure you, dear lady, you are a very good-looking woman. My time with you has been delightful."

Obviously perked by his compliments, she responded in a girlish voice, "Oh, Mr. Thompson, is that really the truth?"

The old man sighed and answered flatly, "No. But there will be plenty of time for the truth when you are emotionally stronger to hear it."[5]

If you are dating a man who exhibits one of these lying habits, run. You will not change him. Marriage will not change him. Only the Lord will change him, and then only when he is willing to acknowledge that he has a dishonesty problem.

If you are married to a man who has a problem telling the truth, then seek help. If your security level is shattered for too long, you will begin to want out of your marriage. Take some necessary steps, and ask yourself some questions about your own truth and trust level. Are you always truthful to your spouse? Is honesty a problem for both of you? Come to the cross. Remember, books, counselors, and therapists are not the answers for your marriage—God is.

Don't be dismayed if you have discovered that either you or your spouse is struggling with one or more of the kinds of lies that I have described in this chapter. It is never too late to make the changes necessary to strengthen the foundation of honesty in your marriage relationship. Many couples struggle with this issue. However, there is no marriage that can survive a continual climate of dishonesty.

Always remember that "honesty is the best marriage insurance policy."

In his book *Love Busters*, Dr. Harley sets forth clearly defined guidelines to keep your relationship pure and honest before your husband and the Lord.[6] Remember that in order *to get* an honest relationship, you *must contribute honesty* to the relationship.

Follow this rule of honesty: reveal to your husband as much information about yourself as you know—your thoughts, feelings, habits, likes, dislikes, personal history, daily activities, and plans for the future.

BE HONEST ABOUT YOUR EMOTIONS

So many times we hear men tell us that we are so much more "emotional" about the events of our lives than they are. Because of that, it is sometimes easier for a wife to keep her emotions hidden from her husband. But it will be difficult for your husband to give you the emotional support that you want and need from him if you cannot openly express your emotions—positive and negative—to him. Dr. Harley describes this as *emotional honesty.*[7] Because you have not given him your *emotional honesty,* he will disappoint you by his lack of understanding of the emotions you are feeling.

I remember when our first wedding anniversary was approaching, I began to have fantasies of what our celebration would be like. I envisioned a surprise candlelight dinner at a romantic restaurant. Maybe he would surprise me with a trip. That would be great!

I began to dream of all the possible places he could take me. I thought about what I would wear and how I would react to such a fabulous surprise.

HE SAYS . . .

If there is anything in your heart, soul, or mind that frustrates you in your marriage relationship toward your spouse, start talking about it today.

Time passed, and nothing was mentioned about a possible celebration. I could hardly stand it. I created my own excitement. Then the day came. My husband walked in the door with a dozen red roses. I looked for the card. "To the most beautiful woman in the world. I love you. Juan."

What! No trip? My husband could tell I was disappointed. "Is something wrong?" he asked, almost afraid of what I would say.

"No, not at all," I responded. "The flowers are beautiful." I was not truthful with my answer. We went to dinner, and a full year passed before I told him what I expected for our first celebration.

The first thing he said to me was, "I didn't know!" How true, because I didn't tell him. I wasn't honest.

Well, baby, that has changed! I am so honest with what I need and want from him now that I write it on the bathroom mirror with lipstick! I leave notes in his briefcase and in the pages of his sermons! Notes are left on his office calendar: "Diana needs a date night—now!"

Satan is present to destroy the works of the Lord in His people. He wants to keep you from communicating honestly with your husband. If you are dishonest, you will be falling right into the evil one's trap to rob, kill, and destroy your marriage.

BE HONEST ABOUT YOUR PAST

After one of my teaching sessions, a beautiful woman requested to speak to me. She waited until the room was almost empty, then she came to me and began to sob uncontrollably. After regaining her composure, she began to tell me about her wonderful ten-year marriage and her great children. As I listened, I could not imagine what the problem was. She finally got the courage to tell me.

Years before she met her husband, she had an affair that resulted in a pregnancy and an abortion. No one knew—including her husband. This event had tormented her for years. Her ultimate fear was that if she told her husband, he would leave her. This form of blackmail is a standard "method of operation" for the devil. I held her until her sobbing subsided, and I prayed with her until I could feel the peace of the Lord overtake her.

I convinced her to tell her husband the truth about her past. I knew the wonderful husband and father she described to me would also have a compassionate heart. I told her that the church was ready to counsel them after the past had been revealed. If she would do this, no longer would Satan hold her hostage to this secret. She agreed.

Within a few days she came to me once again, radiant. She told her husband. She recounted the event and said that her husband's biggest disappointment was in her not trusting him with this traumatic event in her life before this time.

Time passed, and she came to me once more. She told me that after the initial shock of her secret, and because of her repentant spirit before her husband, their relationship was bet-ter than it had ever been before. She felt a free-dom from the past that she had thought would never be possible. She had been delivered from her accuser. The only way to stop paying his ransom was to expose him. This woman and her husband now had a marriage that was pure and honest before each other and the Lord. Make *historical honesty* a part of your relationship with your husband.[8]

Remember that it isn't *honesty* that drives a wedge of distance into your marriage—it is *dis-honesty.* Be willing to share the things in your past that have happened to you, even the things that you consider to be failures or areas of weakness. And allow him to share his past—good and bad—with you.

> ### HE SAYS...
> **Every person in every married relationship makes major mistakes despite the best intentions and all the wisdom in the world.**

BE HONEST ABOUT YOUR PRESENT

How willing are you for your husband to know everything that is happening in your life today? Are there things that you consider "too minor" for him to have to know? Are there things that you have decided he just "doesn't need to know"?

Provide your spouse with a calendar of your activities, giving special emphasis to the things that affect your spouse. Find a time to discuss your day and to give him a chance to tell you about his. Recalling the events of your day allows you to practice *current honesty*.[9]

This is tough—especially for my husband and me. I am a detail person, and I remember things well. These are two traits that men find hard to live with. A third kicker—I want to know everything, and I want to know it right away! My husband has to deal with all three.

To become informed with my daily schedule is enough to choke a horse! I have five kids, four "in-loves," three grandchildren, and eighteen thousand church members. I coordinate the special events of our church, serve as the chief of staff of the television arm of our ministry, and maintain our home, which hosts many social events through the year—and I want to tell my husband everything!

I know that my husband feels there was some peccadillo that he must have committed as a child that caused him to owe such a great penance! I try to relay to him the day's events as we lie in bed at night. I find this ritual to be the best sleep aid he has, for long before my diatribe is over, I hear the sounds of sleep coming from his side of the bed.

On the other hand—and you know there is always another hand—my husband doesn't flow with information as freely as I do. I often find out what is happening in the church through leaders or assistants. That used to bother me a lot. Now it doesn't bother me as much, but since we are talking about honesty, it still bothers me *a little*. Men are wired totally different than women. They can't help it. Things that I consider important he couldn't care less about, and therefore he forgets to tell me about them.

The most important component is honesty. To forget something is not the same thing as avoiding telling me about something or dishonestly relaying the facts to me. If you learn to understand this, it will save you much grief and keep you from many arguments. The longer you are married, the more you will realize this fact: the fewer arguments you have, the better your life will be.

BE HONEST ABOUT YOUR FUTURE

There is something special in sharing the future with the person you love. To sit on the back porch or lie in bed at night in the privacy of your bedroom and reveal your dreams is some of the most intimate honesty you will ever experience. Dreams are sacred ground, never to be taken for granted or belittled.

As you learn to reveal this intimacy with your husband, and he with you, your marriage will go to a new level of trust that you never thought possible. Many men and women don't share this deep side of themselves for fear the person they love will reject their dreams, so many of these hopes and aspirations remain unachieved because they were never acknowledged or communicated.

Revealing your thoughts and plans . . . your hopes and dreams . . . and your goals and aspirations allow you and your husband to experience *future honesty*.[10]

Even the Lord Himself shares His plans with you for the future: "'For I know the plans I have for you,' declares the LORD, 'plans to prosper you and not to harm you, plans to give you hope and a future'" (Jer. 29:11, NIV).

CREATE A CLIMATE OF COMPLETE HONESTY

Too many times I have heard the following phrase at luncheons or similar women's gatherings: "What he doesn't know won't hurt him." To the contrary, it will not only hurt him and his future trust in you, but it will also contribute to the demise of your marriage.

This has never been a problem with me. I was a boring child, never doing anything much of consequence . . . always doing as I was told. I have always had a keen sense of conscience.

My mother kept a Ping-Pong paddle behind the living room couch for the purpose of corporal punishment. When I felt that I did something wrong, I would begin to cry, run to the living room, retrieve the paddle, and run to my mother. I would hand her the paddle, and she would spank me, at which point the level of my cries would increase by several decibels. Then I would return the paddle to its rightful place. To this day,

> **HE SAYS . . .**
>
> **Communication happens when you, as husband and wife, can honestly tell each other who you are, what you think, how you feel, what you love, what you honor, what you esteem, what you hate, and what you fear, desire, hope for, believe in, and are committed to without fear of a prolonged argument.**

neither my mother nor I can remember what my offenses were. The important thing is that I was repentant for them.

My method of operation is still the same. When I have done or said something I feel my husband may not approve of (don't get excited, I'm still the same boring individual), I pick up the phone and open my conversation with, "Honey, I just said something I think you should know about." Why do I do this? Not because I am a "goody-two-shoes," and not because I am afraid of my husband. I do it because I don't want to disappoint him. I don't want anything to get between my cherished relationship with my husband and his trust in me.

Not telling the whole truth is the same as telling a lie. To provide partial information that leads your spouse away from the complete truth is deception. To manipulate the facts to create a false impression is dishonest. Build your marriage on the foundation of *complete honesty*.[11]

HINTS FOR HIM

There is no greater compliment than to be known as *an honest man—* a man of integrity, one who always tells the truth, not just to his wife, but also to his children and to those with whom he is associated.

There is no such thing as a little white lie. Not only do these lies add up to create an image not equal to the image of Christ, but they will also eventually entrap you in the end. A lifetime of integrity can be destroyed by one decision to lie.

A relationship of trust can crumble if you choose to be dishonest with your wife. Don't take that chance. The Bible clearly asks you to choose life and blessing. (See Deuteronomy 30:19.) Maintaining an honest lifestyle before the Lord and your loved ones will always result in long life and bountiful blessings.

My husband often tells the story of John Smith, a loyal carpenter who worked for a very successful building contractor for more than twenty-five years. One day his boss called John into his office and said, "John, my wife and I are leaving for a tour of Europe. We will be gone for six months before I come home and retire. I'm putting you in charge of the last house we build. I want you to order all of the finest materials, including the furnishings, and oversee the job from the ground up."

John accepted the assignment with great enthusiasm and excitement. For ten days before ground was broken at the building site, John studied the blueprints. He checked every measurement, every specification. Suddenly he had a thought. *If I am really in charge, why can't I cut a few corners, use less expensive materials, and put a sizable amount of money into my pocket. No one will know the difference. Once it's painted, it will look like all the other houses.*

John set out on a path he had never traveled before, the road to deception. He ordered second-grade lumber, but his reports indicated that it was top-grade. He ordered inexpensive concrete for the foundation, put in cheap wiring, and cut every corner he could. Yet he reported the purchase of the finest materials.

When the home was completed and fully painted, he asked his employer to come and inspect it. "John," the contractor said, "what a magnificent job you have done! You have been such a good, honest, and loyal friend and carpenter all these years that I have decided to show my gratitude by giving you this house you built as a gift for a token of my appreciation!"[12]

The truth will find you out. The Word of God warns that what we do in secret He will shout from the housetops.

> There is nothing concealed that will not be disclosed, or hidden that will not be made known. What you have said in the dark will be heard in the daylight, and what you have whispered in the ear in the inner rooms will be proclaimed from the roofs.
>
> —LUKE 12:2–3, NIV

Remember, the Lord your Creator knows your heart. He records the words of your mouth. To be known as an honest man by your wife, children, and loved ones is the greatest testimony you will have and the greatest legacy you will leave.

FROM DR. ANNE

If there is a single quality that has major impact on the building up, as well as tearing down, of marriage, it is *honesty*. This is a many-sided value that will make or break a marriage.

Honesty is a character strength that women say they want in their husbands, but this strength can be the most frustrating quality their husbands possess. Honesty must be carefully defined—especially from God's point of view.

"Being honest" should never be confused with being brutal and uncompassionate. An honest person does not compromise his or her values by tempering honesty with qualities of care, consideration, and tactfulness. Remember that husbands are to love their wives just as God loves the church. God never abuses.

There isn't a woman alive who hasn't asked her husband, "Does my hair look all right?" or "Does this dress look OK for tonight?"

Hurt feelings will be avoided and your husband will still be honest if he replies, "I think you are so beautiful. You know, you have another style I like better." God shows us mercy and is gracious to us. Shouldn't we be gracious and merciful to each other? This should be particularly true for the mate that God has given us. Find a way to respond to your mate with honesty that is offered with gracious, compassionate, and loving balance.

Honesty is *balanced* by the tact and compassion that we see modeled by Jesus Christ Himself. The love that Jesus had for those to whom He ministered was reflected in His statements and personal position. He never compromised truth, but He didn't purpose to hurt or destroy—only to shed light.

How honest are you as a woman of God? Are you strong enough to receive and accept leadership that is uncompromising and honest? Will you be honest with *yourself* as well as with your husband? Or will you bare your fangs and hiss when his *honesty* doesn't agree with what you wanted to hear?

There are two persons involved in every verbal transaction involving honesty. One is the person who is being honest with you—and the other is *you!* Every marriage will need both people in that marriage to be committed totally to honesty—whether in the position of expressing an honest opinion or statement, or receiving the expression from his or her mate.

A man with honesty is governed by a sense of right and wrong, which is not swayed by a whim, even his wife's whims. He is not easily manipulated by circumstances or ego. When he is away, he isn't subject to corruption by peer pressure or social conformity.

He doesn't lie to his wife or to others. He is correct in his morals and conduct.

Balance in all of the marriage qualities, including honesty, encourages and elevates without compromising the facts. Honesty, combined with the companion characteristics of compassion, encouragement, and support, builds confidence and trust.

Ladies, use wisely every opportunity you have to elevate and support your husband. Your husband *does* care what you think about him. Based on your responses to him, he will go to work feeling like a winner or a loser. Follow the example of Christ, who ministered to each person He met in truth balanced with grace and compassion.

CLOSING PRAYERS

Why be held captive to the ways of the world? Embrace the freedom of truth. The Word of God tells us that the knowledge of the truth will set us free—free from the chains of the past and free from the fear of tomorrow. There is nothing so liberating as the truth. Truth must have a covenant with love, and honesty must be intertwined with trust, in order for the union of holy matrimony to succeed.

PRAYER OF REPENTANCE

Father God, I lied today, and I am so sorry. I have lied a lot lately. I have almost made it a way of life. I make up a story so I can avoid trouble and conflict. I am not straightforward with my husband. Yet I demand honesty from him. I lie by not telling him things he really should be told. I sometimes manipulate the truth by exaggerating or minimizing the facts. I am also guilty of asking questions that I know will cause an argument if he is honest with his answers. I have not been truthful with him about my needs and desires, and I have later accused him of not meeting them. I call on Your forgiveness, Lord. I know that I can begin anew and turn from my past as I repent before You and those I have hurt.

PRAYER OF NEW BEGINNINGS

Lord Jesus, I want to be one with my husband as You are one with the Father. I will not lie to my husband about my feelings, my needs, and my desires. I pledge to be forthright and honest. I will be kind and gentle in my conversation with my husband so he can respond to me in the fashion I long for. I want to share all that I am with him, as I share all that I am with You. I want him to feel secure in being honest with me. Together we can take our needs to You in prayer. I want to grow closer to my husband each day as our lives are a reflection of the example You have set. I want my husband to trust me, and I want to trust him. This will be an example of our love and devotion to You and one another. I praise and honor You, my God. I can't do this without You. I desire to please You. I want the desire of my heart to be pure and to be reflected in the words that come from my lips. Amen.

> My son, if your heart is wise, then my heart will be
> glad; my inmost being will rejoice when your lips
> speak what is right.
>
> —PROVERBS 23:15–16, NIV

WOMEN OFTEN FALSELY accuse men of not listening. We know they can hear us all right—they are just not paying attention. Actually, this is a gift. A man can follow the moves of a graceful quarterback on the turf while watching TV or track the path of a little white ball on the green until it falls in a shallow hole, all the while nodding and occasionally delivering a "hmmm," while his wife is having a passionate, cathartic, one-sided conversation with him.

I have come to the conclusion that men are truly different. The old adage says, "Thank God for the difference!" As women, it is important to identify the differences *and* acknowledge that *God* created most of these differences. We have no business changing that which God has ordained. But we must learn to adapt to these differences.

When I was newly married, I attended a Bible study taught by an older lady in the church. She told the young group of women that if we wanted to change certain characteristics in our husbands, we should pray. Eventually, God would make the changes we desired.

I was sure what she was saying had to be right on target—after all, she was an older woman! I thought, *Wow! My mother never told me this!* I went directly home, made my "Change Order," and submitted it to God.

I put my wish list in my Bible and prayed over it every day. "Lord, make my husband more spontaneous and less methodical. Make him more flexible and less rigid. Make him want to smell the roses and not trample over them." Every day I prayed and waited for *the change*.

One morning the answer came. Now, I must tell you that I am not a "woo...woo..." kind of person. I don't hear the voice of God audibly. I don't see colorful pictures in my head. Yet I am sensitive to the Holy Spirit who lives inside of me, and I try to listen to His voice when He speaks.

On this morning, as I was praying a thought came to my mind: *Today you will receive the man you have been praying for. I will make the changes in him you have requested.* Because this thought came out of the blue, I knew it was God. I was excited. I thought, *That wasn't difficult at all!* As I was celebrating my answered prayer, another thought came just as unexpectedly as the first. It seemed God wasn't finished: *Today, I will give you the husband you want—but then I can no longer use him.*

My celebration turned to spontaneous humility. I began to weep. I knelt on the floor and asked God to forgive me. My husband no longer used of God? I could hardly stand it! "Because of me! Please, Lord, no!" I prayed fervently. After my time of repentance was complete, the sweet presence of the Holy Spirit comforted me as He began to show me how He used the traits He put in my husband for His purposes.

The methodical approach he has for life is what God molds into the discipline needed for the hours of study and preparation of the Word of God. It enables my husband to present his message to the sheep of His pasture every Sunday. His rigid stance is the strength he must draw from when standing on the uncompromising message of the gospel of Jesus Christ. The determination that drives him is the tenacity the Creator put in him to fight injustice and stand for good, no matter what the cost. I wanted to change that which the Creator put into him for His purposes. I was the one who needed to change.

MEN COMMUNICATE DIFFERENTLY THAN WOMEN

We want our husbands to communicate with us in the same way we communicate with other women. They can't. Bill Cosby said, "Women don't want to hear what you [men] think. Women want to hear what they think, in a deeper voice." Men want women to be content with the quality of communication they have with other men. We won't be.

We all know the stereotypes: men dominate the remote control and relish in the power they have as they surf through the channels, while women enjoy watching the commercials. When men are under pressure, they brood or go to a hockey game and scream for blood. Women eat chocolates and go shopping. A man can go into a room full of people and leave after two hours, not knowing a soul. A woman can go into a public bathroom and make friends with a perfect stranger as they compare the makeup they use. We are different!

> HE SAYS...
>
> **Women enjoy the process of reaching a goal. Men want to get to the goal as soon as possible—forget the process.**

My husband finds it hard to remember that when we were courting we would spend several hours on the phone every evening. I, of course, remember it all. It is a sweet, romantic memory of our past. When I ask him to tell me more about himself and what he is thinking, his response is: "I've told you everything there is to know about me! It was different then."

Different, yet the same. The same time, effort, and attention it took for a man to court his wife is the same he needs to keep her feeling secure and happy within the marriage relationship.

Communication is meant to be a blessing in marriage, not a torment. When I hear the jokes about communication between men and women, I conclude that marriage is both: a blessing for the woman and a torment for the man. It doesn't have to be this way. When seen through the eyes of love, communication is the lifeline for any marriage.

COMMUNICATION RULES

An old adage says, "It's better *felt* than *telt!*" There are some communication rules that I want to share with you that demonstrate the truth of learning to communicate *through experience.* Some of the experiences that teach us good communication with our spouses are positive, "right-on" examples of how to do communication the right way. Others are ... well, others teach us how to communicate *the next time* in a far better way than we did *the last time.*

As I let you into the life of my husband and me in the following paragraphs, you will see that we too have learned from experience. Perhaps after sharing this experience with us, you will decide to incorporate these communication rules into your own life. Take it from me... they work!

Communication rule: Communication is not nagging or boasting.

When my husband and I decided to make our first trip to Israel, we were very excited. I was four months pregnant with our son Matthew, but nonetheless eager and ready for the trip. This was going to be a second honeymoon experience for us. I had no idea how long the trip would take. We were not the seasoned travelers we are now. My husband, being the determined man he is, made the decision to go to Israel one Sunday evening. The following Monday morning, he called New York to begin making arrangements for what would be a life-changing experience.

He began his phone conversation with these words: "New York, I want to go to Israel on the next tour out!" We were booked by the end of the day. We began our journey less than one month later by leaving San Antonio and flying to Houston. From Houston we flew to New York, from New York to Amsterdam, from Amsterdam to Athens, Greece, and from Athens to Lanarca, Cyprus. Once in Cyprus, we boarded a Greek liner and began a voyage across the Mediterranean Sea to Port Said, Egypt. After three days in Egypt, we boarded the ship once again and sailed into the beautiful Port of Haifa, Israel.

Are you tired yet? I was. By the time we boarded the ship in Cyprus, we had already been traveling thirty-six hours! I was exhausted. The story gets better.

Communication rule: "If Momma ain't happy, ain't nobody happy!"

We boarded the liner, which was not exactly the *Love Boat,* I might add. We had difficulty finding our room. We asked several crewmembers for directions, but most of them did not speak English. Finally, one of them understood us sufficiently to lead us to the floor above the boiler room. You guessed it; our room was directly over the boiler room. My husband opened the door, and I walked into the room, quickly observing that the place intended for our second honeymoon had no bed.

"John, this room has no bed!" I announced as if it was some brilliant deduction.

"Yes, it does, honey," my husband answered, staring at one of the tiny room's four walls.

"No," I responded, "I see no bed. They must have us in the wrong room!"

With that, John walked to the wall and pulled two straps that were hanging suspiciously from the wall. Suddenly, as if produced from thin air, two bunk beds appeared in the room.

My mouth fell open. He looked at me and made what I thought was a very imprudent remark. "I'll flip you for the top bunk!" I stared holes through him as I held my pregnant belly in such a way to make sure he realized that I was the woman who was carrying his child and that I was not very happy at the moment.

> **HE SAYS...**
>
> **Conflicting expectations are the source of most unhappiness in marriage.**

"I was only kidding! I'll help you strap into bed," he responded sympathetically, trying to make amends for what he now considered to be a foolish proposal.

Communication rule: Good communication is *quality*, not quantity.

As my husband climbed into the top bunk, I lay there remembering my last encounter on the high seas. It was not a pleasant memory. We had taken what became known as the *infamous Hagee family fishing trip* in the Texas Gulf three years earlier. Unbeknownst to my husband or me, I was also with child at that time. I had never been on the ocean before, and I was not feeling well at all. The nausea I felt was overwhelming. I know I hold the record for the *Guinness Book of World Records* for chumming—at least eight hours! It was not an amusing experience.

Now on this first trip to Israel, I was about to embark on my second high sea voyage. I became worried and was prompted by my fears to ask my husband for help.

I called out to my husband, who had just positioned himself in the narrow berth above me, "Honey, I need you to pray that I will not get seasick."

Rather impatiently, he replied, "You won't get sick. It's all in your mind. Don't think about it, and you will go straight to sleep."

"I don't care where it is!" was my determined comeback. "I need you to pray for it, wherever it is! I want you to pray that I will not get seasick!"

The prayer that came from my husband's mouth was not what I had in mind. "Dear Lord, keep my wife from getting seasick. Amen."

"That's no prayer!" I shouted. "Why, that didn't even clear the ceiling!"

John was aggravated now. "Look, Diana, it had to clear the ceiling, because my nose is touching the ceiling!"

I couldn't leave well enough alone. "John Hagee, I need you to pray a real prayer!" I issued my demand, and, much to my disgust, I could hear the sounds of snoring coming from above. He was asleep! How dare he?

This story is a classic example of the communication differences between a man and a woman. I wanted a bodacious prayer, a long, powerful, bring-the-house-down, Charlton Heston, part-the-Red-Sea kind of prayer! He wanted to be more prudent. A quick and to the point prayer for him was sufficient.

My husband feels God needs no pleading; He just requires faith—imagine that! I was too exhausted to wake him, and to continue the argument over a prayer for healing somehow didn't seem right.

The ship began to rock as it embarked on its journey across the Mediterranean. Bored, I began to purvey the tiny space we were in. I adjusted my eyes to the dim light coming from the miniscule porthole. There was one single dresser in the room, positioned right next to my narrow bed. The other end of the dresser rested against the opposite wall of that little room.

There were two doors to our "stateroom with an ocean view." One led to the hall, and the other to the bathroom. The only other furnishings were the two berths, which pushed up into the wall during the day. We were definitely in tight quarters. Finally, the rocking of the ship, coupled with the serenade of the engine below us and the sounds of slumber coming from my husband, put me sound to sleep, a miracle in its own right.

Communication rule: Don't speak without thinking about the full nature of the consequences.

Suddenly, I was awakened from my deep "miracle sleep" by the thud of my head tapping against the dresser, which was sandwiched between my cot and the wall. From the captain's announcement later, we learned that we were in the roughest storm he had ever experienced in his career. As my mind became clearer, I could hear sounds coming from the "naval latrine." I listened closely and soon realized that it was the sound of my husband upchucking his dinner.

This is true confession time. When I heard that sound, I thought of what it represented, and I immediately began to feel it was vindication for the halfhearted prayer my husband had offered for me earlier that night. I called out from my bunk, "Honey, are you sick?"

No response.

"John, do you need my help?" No decipherable answer came from the bathroom, just continued gagging.

I went to the door of the room ready to say boastfully, "I told you so!" But instantly I felt compassion for the man lying in front of the metal bowl anchored to the floor. It was not a pretty sight. His legs and arms wrapped around the latrine as if it were his life jacket; his head was positioned deep into the bowl. All I could hear were sounds of muffled gagging interrupted only by his gasps for air. Without thinking I said, "Guess what? Your prayer worked, and I'm not even nauseous!"

You can imagine the look that came from his red face, and I knew that he would later have to repent for his thoughts.

Communication rule: Timing is everything.

I quietly backed out of the small cubbyhole and sat on the narrow bed until the sounds of retching stopped. He came out of the room and began to dress. I was shocked, because it was barely four in the morning of God only knows what time zone we were in. "Where in the world are you going?" I asked.

"I'm going to ask the captain how long before we are off this tub!" was his aggravated response. I sat on the edge of my bunk, which by now gave me a small sense of security, and remained there until his return. As he walked back into the room, I asked him cautiously what the outcome of his visit had been. "Eight more lousy, stinking hours!" he railed.

He took the bedding off the top bunk and laid it on the floor next to my bed. I got into my cot. As he lay there on the floor, he reached for my hand. I took it and held it tightly. Of all the things I felt I had the right to say, and all the things I could have said, I chose to softly whisper, "I love you."

"I love you, too," was his tender response. Our second honeymoon had finally begun.

> **HE SAYS...**
>
> **Through sickness and health, for richer and poorer, marriage requires devotion and a mature ability to commit when it's the last thing you want to do.**

PRAYER—THE BEST COMMUNICATION TOOL

I could go on and on and recount several books written about communication by qualified counselors, but, if needed, you can read these books on your own. What I do want to share with you is what I have found to be the best form of communication you will ever experience with your spouse. It is the communication you have in prayer with each other and with God.

The Lord uses communication to maintain a lifeline to His people. He uses several forms of communication. One is His written Word. Another is His voice, which is manifested through our conscience. He speaks to us through His people, who are the hands and feet of the living God. We, in turn, communicate to our Father in supplication, in praise, and in worship. Without participation in these forms of communication, the Christian will become distant from God, and his soul will soon dry and wither.

When we come to Him united, in one accord, as husband and wife, and lay our needs at His altar, our Lord makes a promise to us. Jesus is the Promise Keeper of all promise keepers:

> Again I tell you, if two of you on earth agree (harmonize together, make a symphony together) about whatever [anything and everything] they may ask, it will come to pass and be done for them by My Father in heaven.
> —MATTHEW 18:19, AMP

Can you imagine? *Anything and everything!* The operative words in this promise are "agree," "harmonize," and "symphony." What beautiful music we must make in the heavenlies when we pray together with our spouses in unity!

When my husband and I pray together, we get answers from heaven. And it is simply not possible to be angry with one another when you pray!

> For this reason I am telling you, whatever you ask for in prayer, believe (trust and be confident) that it is granted to you, and you will [get it]. And whenever you stand praying, if you have anything against anyone, forgive him and let it drop (leave it, let it go), in

order that your Father Who is in heaven may also forgive you your [own] failings and shortcomings and let them drop.
—MARK 11:24–25, AMP

Find a private time and place for prayer. Satan will make sure that the phone will ring, your children will scream for you, or the doorbell will ring. My husband and I like to have our prayer time while we walk. We are away from intrusions and able to call on the Lord in freedom. I am sure you and your husband can find a place and time on which you can agree.

Make a prayer list. My husband and I have prayed together for almost thirty years; therefore, it is engraved in our minds. First, we come into a time of repentance, asking forgiveness for anything we have said, done, or thought that has grieved the Holy Spirit. Our list then begins: We pray for our children by name, their spouses, and our grandchildren—those already here and those to come. We pray for the protection, direction, and prosperity of our church, television outreach, and school, and for everyone associated with them. Then we submit any personal petitions we may have. Finally, we pray for the peace of Jerusalem and end in a time of praise for our Lord and His blessings.

Learn to pray in *agreement*, not in competition. There is no sweeter sound in the heavens than the sound of a husband and wife in harmony before the throne of God. There is nothing more powerful.

The more this divine communication occurs, the more you will want to talk to each other about other things. You will find that the "things" you speak about with your spouse will not include gossip or tale bearing. Your conversation will concentrate on the petitions that you put before the Lord and the testimonies associated with those prayers. With your husband you will share the dreams and aspirations each of you has as together you come into agreement. Your children will know that when Mom and Dad pray, things happen. This teaching is far greater than any book or class you will ever enroll them in. Without communication, your marriage will wither and become dry, just like the soul when it has no time with God.

HINTS FOR HIM

In the leadership chapter of this book, I made a statement about a woman submitting to a husband's lead and a man submitting to a wife's need. Both men and women need communication. As the leader of the household, it is important that you understand the importance of communicating to your wife.

HINT #1: There is nothing sweeter than your wife hearing these words coming from you: "Honey, I'm home. I can hardly wait to tell you about my day! How did your day go today?" It sure beats dragging information out of you, which forces your wife into the role of interrogator.

HINT #2: Your wife would love a "just because" telephone call from you. End this call with "I love you, and I bless you in the name of the Lord." When expressions of love are unsolicited, they are invaluable.

HINT #3: Listen. Women need to be listened to just as much as men do. One of the greatest gifts you can give your wife is your undivided attention. I know your time is precious, and she does, too.

HINT #4: Just as with God, communication comes in many forms. Some men find it difficult to express their feelings in conversation. Some of the most beautiful forms of communication are handwritten letters. I keep the letters, cards, and notes my husband has given me through the years in a special drawer, and when I need a special blessing, I go to the file and make a little withdrawal of all the love stored and deposited on those pages. They are priceless to me.

HINT #5: Other forms of communication that women love are what I call "love pats" or "love smiles." This can take place at any time of the day or night. They can be in private or in public. They are simply special personal ways you let each other know you care. Remember, some of the most treasured investments you will make in your wife cost you nothing.

HINT #6: *Let it drop!* Take heed to what the Lord instructs His people. In order to qualify to come to His throne in supplication, you must leave your offenses and let them go! If not, you won't be heard. No exceptions!

As you meet your wife's needs through the communion of your heart with hers, you will help to make your marriage the beautiful union God intended it to be.

FROM DR. ANNE

Communication is the *sharing* of ideas. This can involve two people or one person gaining knowledge from an outside source. Communication is also *expressing* ideas. True communication is a *dialogue,* not merely a monologue. Communication happens when one person is speaking and the other person is listening.

Some women have a habit of talking incessantly, hardly pausing for breath or to allow dialogue. They pause only long enough to reload for another assault. Do you want your husband to "communicate"? If you do, it requires your husband giving feedback to your monologue. That's what turns the monologue into dialogue.

Communication is more than an echo of your own opinion. A differing opinion should not spark an argument. Opinions that are different will not shut down communication as long as there are communication rules that are respected by both husband and wife. Allow time for both of you to be heard without interruption. When an argument arises, give each other permission to take a timeout from the discussion. Set a time when both of you will return to the conversation. Determine that during the timeout, neither of you will attempt to discuss the subject about which you were in disagreement.

When I am counseling couples about the issue of communication, I give each person the following list of rules:

- No name calling.
- Never attack the person—only the subject.
- Never use violence.
- Always give the opportunity to rephrase the last statement.
- Always pay attention.
- Never interrupt.
- Stick to the subject.
- Set an appointment for a subject requiring serious discussion (this avoids distractions).

- If the discussion goes too long, set a time several days later to continue the discussion.

How much conversation, information, and talk are enough? When is the best time to share quality time? When you have both had a challenging day and are shifting gears from the day's work as you enter the common place you share (probably your home), that is NOT a good time to unload problems or demand answers.

Both of you need to use wisdom and allow the other to have "reentry time." A quiet environment is unbelievably calming. Decompression won't take long if you both cooperate. Children should see this time as calm family time, not as a contest for attention from both parents.

Genuine love and communication are not defined by an emotional experience. An emotional experience cannot seal your relationship with your husband or with your Father in heaven. If the Word of God doesn't have lordship in your life, then God is not the Lord of your life.

Our desire for an intimate relationship with our spouses is a God-given desire. It can't be accomplished without knowing the motivations, thoughts, or ways of your spouse. Jesus said, "I and My Father are one" (John 10:30). His Father's thoughts and ways had been communicated to Him. Jesus spent time in sweet communion and communication with God. Jesus spoke to God. God spoke to Jesus. They shared a common heart, vision, and love.

Do you place a priority on the time you spend with God? With your husband? Do you value the time you spend with your husband? Make this your goal, and see if your communication with your husband doesn't drastically improve.

CLOSING PRAYERS

It is no coincidence that the word *communicate* derives from the word *commune*, which means "to converse intimately, to give and receive or have Holy Communion." To give of each other by sharing each other's thoughts and dreams in an unselfish manner, looking for no gain in return other than a closer relationship with the one you love, is one of the most precious expressions of love you can give to your spouse.

PRAYER OF REPENTANCE

Lord, I get very lonely sometimes. I forget that You too get lonely for my voice as well. Forgive me for not talking to You more. I know if I repent before You, it will cancel those things I have done that have brought disappointment to You. Forgive me, Lord. I ask also that You forgive me for the times I have spoken to my husband in critical, nagging, and accusing tones that I know will not edify him, strengthen our relationship, or be a good example of my relationship with You. I have also been guilty of not listening to him when he is trying to talk to me about his needs or desires. I ask for Your forgiveness. I want my own needs met, and I am not sensitive to hearing his thoughts and needs. Help me, Lord, to calm my thinking and to communicate my feelings without the cloud of my emotions. I need to talk with my husband about good things, those things that are beautiful, and bring hope to our future. Help me to make this happen. Amen.

PRAYER OF NEW BEGINNINGS

First of all, Lord, allow me to give You praise for the opportunity of beginning anew. A fresh start is what I need. I have read in Your Word, my Father God, and I know that it reflects Your desire to communicate with me. You want to hear my petitions, and You want me to listen as You answer my prayers. I am so grateful. Help me, Lord, to apply the rules that define my communication with You and my communication with my husband. I vow to be still and know without a doubt that You are my God. I vow to be still and listen to the words and thoughts my husband is conveying to me. I will apply his words to the knowledge I have of him and his ways. I know You and Your ways. Help me to understand my husband's communication to me. I know he is trying, and together, with Your help, we will start fresh and have a new attitude about our communication with each other. I will, with Your help, forgive him for hurting me. I will "drop it" and come to You with a pure heart. I will pray with my husband in one accord, as together we approach Your throne in harmony. I thank You, Father, for being there for me and mine whenever we call upon Your name. You are so precious to me. Amen.

eight

Want Number Three:
SENSE OF HUMOR

A happy heart is good medicine and a cheerful mind works healing, but a broken spirit dries up the bones.

—PROVERBS 17:22, AMP

HUMOR IS DEFINED in various ways. Humor can describe anything from a person's temperament, mood, and state of mind to a person's ability to express or appreciate what is funny or amusing.

Life is too short not to be filled with laughter and good times. Then again, laughter and good times are many things to many people. In his book titled *Being Happy in an Unhappy World*, my husband describes many things that happiness is not.[1]

I know that women are not looking for the eternal comedian. I have been around men who are actually extremely gifted at making other people laugh. However, a little goes a long way, and after a while, you are ready for serious and meaningful conversation. You can often look deep into the eyes of individuals who have to be the life of the party and see a sadness that does not fit with their outward façade. It is very difficult to have a great sense of humor without being a happy person.

Some people just don't have a talent for humor. I, for example, have a quick wit, but I couldn't tell a joke successfully if you paid me. On the other hand, my husband has both talents. Our children all have quick minds and a great sense of humor, and our times together are often hilarious. However, I know from visiting in other households that not all families have this in common.

Humor is not laughing at someone else's expense. I've been in social gatherings where the husband or wife is making fun of his or her spouse in some sort of demeaning way. The one making the jokes may be the center of attraction for the moment, but I always look at the person who is the target of the humor. That person may be laughing on the outside, but often he or she is trying to keep from crying.

> **HE SAYS . . .**
>
> **It's important to laugh together, not *at* each other, but *with* each other.**

A HAPPY PERSON DEFINED

Who is a happy person? I know that women, and men, are looking for a person with whom they can enjoy life, a mate who will look at the bright side of things even when the circumstances are not exactly conducive to laughter. In His Word, the Lord gives us the answer to this question by listing at least nine kinds of people who are happy. (See Matthew 5:1–12.)

1. Happy are the humble.

When my mother-in-law married my father-in-law, she was an accomplished Bible teacher and conference speaker. She had speaking engagements booked for years in advance. She loved to teach the Word of God, and she did so with a power and anointing that was electrifying.

My in-laws made the decision to begin a church in Channelview, Texas. She fulfilled the engagements she had for the rest of the calendar year and humbly canceled those for subsequent years.

As she pastored the church with her husband, she realized that her talent for speaking drew larger crowds than her husband. She made the decision to retire from the pulpit to see her husband's ministerial potential realized.

After my father-in-law had gone to heaven, she shared with me the blessings of answered prayer she had received regarding her decision to retire from teaching the Word of God, something I knew she loved. Her decision to stop teaching had not been an easy one. When she came to the conclusion to bring that part of her life to a close, she had a long conversation with the Lord. She shared with Him her desire.

"Lord, as I lay down my ministry to help develop my husband's, I want you to give me a son who will take up the banner of the gospel. I want him to preach to this nation and the nations of the world. I want to have the privilege of witnessing this in my lifetime."

My mother-in-law has a very unique relationship with the Lord. When she speaks, He listens. He knows her heart. He knows her love for Him. He knows the dedication she has for the things of God.

Over sixty-four years later, at ninety-one years of age, she is witnessing the life of her son, my husband, as he preaches the good news of Jesus Christ to this nation and the nations of the world. This winter, with God's help, he will be going to Nigeria, where he will preach for more than two million people each night. Who would have thought!

Vada Hagee would have thought. She humbly laid down her gift. She humbly forfeited her desire to preach the Word of God. She humbly made a request of her God. She had faith in a God who never fails.

She received the desire of her heart. She is oh, so happy as she listens to her son and her grandson Matthew preach the gospel of Jesus Christ as she eagerly awaits the Lord's angels to escort her to her heavenly home. God granted her a double portion.

2. Happy are those who mourn.

Who are those who mourn? Does that only describe those who grieve for the passing of a loved one? We know that our Savior gives peace that surpasses understanding to those who grieve.

No, mourning means more than expressing grief over death or other human tragedy. It refers to those who express sorrow for sin. In short, those who mourn are those who repent before the Lord with tears of brokenness.

Years ago in America, the altar was called "the mourner's bench." It was there, Sunday after Sunday, that those who heard the gospel of Jesus Christ would kneel and confess their sins. That wooden altar was stained from one end to the other with tears worth their weight in gold.

To repent you must take an honest look at yourself and admit that you did wrong. You must feel remorse for your actions and resolve never to repeat those actions again.

To repent before God is one of the most beautiful acts of submission you will ever commit. Rebbetzin Jungreis tells a story of a man described in the Talmud by the name of Eleazar.

He was known as the most immoral man of all time. One day in the company of a prostitute, he experienced a moment of truth when she accused him of being beyond hope, saying he would surely spend eternity in hell.

He was shocked! If a woman of such ill repute accused him of immorality, then he must find help. He ran from her home and called on the hills and the mountains to plead on his behalf. But there was only silence.

He called on heaven and earth for mercy, and there was only silence. He turned to the stars and constellations, begging them to intercede on his behalf, but they too were silent.

Eleazar finally determined that the matter rested entirely with him. He was the only one who could plead his cause, and he repented before his Creator. Suddenly, a heavenly voice was heard, "Eleazar, repentance is accepted!"[2]

Rebbetzin Jungreis goes on to explain the symbolism of the story. The hills and the mountains were Eleazar's parents. He tried to shift the blame for his corruption and his immoral acts to his parents, but the heavenly courts would not accept his rationalization.

Next he blamed the heavens and the earth—which symbolized his environment, his school, and his friends, but that too was rejected. Finally, he turned to the stars and the constellations, which symbolized the bad fate that life had dealt him. His pleading was met with no response.

He finally found the courage and the strength of character to repent before the Lord as King David did: "Father, I have sinned before You and You alone! I must accept full responsibility for my actions!" Repentance was granted, and Eleazar was a happy man.[3]

For the man or woman who has sinned before God, no amount of good humor or tasteless jokes can substitute for the happiness we feel when we mourn for our wrong actions and repent before the Lord.

The Lord describes this happiness as being the result of experiencing God's favor and especially conditioned by the revelation of His matchless grace.[4] This makes for true happiness, my friends.

3. Happy are the patient.

Bishop Charles Blake of West Angeles Church of God in Christ tells the story of the mule that had served his master for years. The mule was now old, and one day the mule fell into a deep pit. The selfish, evil master felt the mule was not worth the feed to sustain him or the bullet it would take to kill him, so the farmer decided to pile garbage over the mule, hoping he would soon be buried in an avalanche of trash and die.

The mule, refusing to yield to the fate of his evil master, shook off the garbage as it was piled upon his back. Then he would stomp on it, pack it down, and wait patiently.

Every day the evil taskmaster would pour more and more garbage on the mule. Every day the faithful mule would shake off the garbage, stomp on the debris, and wait patiently.

Finally the farmer told his neighbors to dump all their garbage in the pit, hoping this would be the demise of the stubborn mule. No matter the amount of garbage that was tossed his way, the mule was methodical in his response. He would shake off the garbage, stomp on it, pack it down, and wait patiently.

One day the farmer and his friends threw one too many loads of garbage! The persistent mule shook off the garbage, stomped on it, and used the debris for an escalator to the top. The trash became his doorway to freedom!

Life is not always fair. Many times we find ourselves in the deepest pits of despair, but as Corrie ten Boom so eloquently stated, "There is no pit so deep that Jesus is not deeper still."

Patience is a virtue, and to wait on God and His provision for our needs will never be without reward. Scripture describes happiness for the patient man or woman as joyous and spiritually prosperous. It brings life filled with joy and satisfaction in God's favor and salvation, regardless of the outward conditions.[5]

4. Happy are those who desire righteousness.

Righteousness is only attained through the blood of Jesus Christ. It's by His sacrifice that His white robe of purity is put over every sinner at the cross. We cannot earn our righteousness; it is freely given. Happy are those who "hunger" for righteousness.

Hungering to do those things that please God is something I believe He acknowledges from His throne in the heavenlies. When we are obedient to His Word, it brings Him pleasure. In His Word He has promised that "gladness and joy will overtake" us if we obey His commandments (Isa. 51:11, NIV).

We may not always be successful in our efforts to please Him, but the sincerity with which we try must be pure.

There is a story about a Jewish family that was deported to the ghettos of Poland in World War II during the regime of Nazi Germany. Of all the lack they suffered, they missed the teaching of the Word of God the most. The father of the family, along with the community leaders, managed to continue teaching the Torah to their children. Desiring to be obedient to the commandment of the Lord to care for the widows and the orphans, the mother did her best to feed all those she could from the meager rations the family received.

Finally they were deported to the Bergen-Belsen concentration camp. Under the most brutalizing conditions, the father continued to teach the Torah to his children. As Rosh Hashanah approached, the rabbis of the camp gathered the people who hungered for the Word of God and amassed three hundred cigarettes, which carried an enormous amount of value in the black market. They did not buy food to celebrate the holiday; instead, they purchased a holiday prayer book and a shofar.

The sound of the shofar brought all that recognized the call to worship near the barbed-wire fence that bordered the camp. The Nazis came running. When they reached the young men who were blowing the ancient horn, they beat them without mercy. As they were being beaten, the men cried unto God: "Blessed art thou, our God, who has commanded us to listen to the sound of the shofar."[6]

These young men were not entirely successful at calling the righteous to prayer, but their desire to obey God's commandments was pure.

In the modern church, pastors are forced to cancel evening services because their members don't attend. Weekend services are added to their worship times, not to accommodate the masses but in hopes of drawing them to the house of God at a more convenient time. This is not hungering for righteousness.

The Scripture promises that those who hunger and thirst for righteousness will be spiritually prosperous in the state in which the born-again child of God enjoys His favor and His salvation.

> **HE SAYS . . .**
> **Ask yourself this question: "Am I truly happy?" If not, why not? The answer lies within yourself.**

They shall be completely satisfied as they yearn to be right standing with God.[7]

5. Happy are those who show mercy.

To have mercy is to show kindness and to forgive. A young man secretly misappropriated several hundreds of dollars from the firm for which he was working. When the action was discovered, the young man was asked to report to the office of the CEO of the company.

As he neared the office of the senior member of the firm, the young man was heavy hearted. He was certain he was about to lose his job. He feared legal action against him. His whole world was collapsing around him, as he was about to receive what he justly deserved.

Once in the office, the CEO questioned the young man about the whole incident.

"Are you guilty of the accusation?" the senior officer asked in a very straightforward manner.

"Yes, sir, I am. I take full responsibility, and I am very sorry for my actions," the young man answered in as strong a voice as he could produce.

Suddenly the executive asked a question that totally shocked the repentant young man. "If I decide to keep you in your present position, do you think I can trust you in the future?"

Shocked, yet without hesitation, the young man lit up with hope and said, "Yes, sir, most definitely; I have learned my lesson!"

The executive continued to share more about his decision. "I have decided not to press charges, and you can keep your job in your present position."

He ended his meeting by telling the young man something that would change his life forever. "I think you ought to know, however, that you are the second man in this firm who succumbed to temptations and was shown leniency. I was the first. What you have done, I did. The mercy you are receiving, I received. It is only the grace of God that can keep us both."[8]

There is a mercy bank in all of our lives. The more you deposit mercy into your bank, the more you will receive when you need to make a withdrawal.

6. Happy are those with a pure heart.

The psalmist asks the question:

Who shall go up into the mountain of the Lord? Or who shall stand in His Holy Place? He who has clean hands and a pure heart, who has not lifted himself up to falsehood or to what is false, nor sworn deceitfully. He shall receive blessing from the Lord and righteousness from the God of his salvation.

—PSALM 24:3–5, AMP

There is nothing so pure as truth and honesty coming from a child. Oh, to keep that kind of purity through our lifetimes. Several years ago we had the privilege of having a "giant" of the evangelical world spend the night in our home. Oral Roberts was spending time with my husband, and we were privileged to have him stay in our guest room. What treasured memories I have of this humble servant of God in my kitchen, commenting on the wonderful aroma of the pot of beans I was cooking for supper. It was a great visit.

I remember, as if it were yesterday, that just before his departure, Dr. Roberts gathered my husband, the children who were home, and myself around him for a prayer of blessing. We assembled in a circle and held hands, bowed our heads, and closed our eyes. I was overflowing with anticipation.

He prayed as only Oral Roberts can pray—powerfully! When the prayer was finished, my eyes were filled with tears, and the peace of God filled our home. Without warning he turned to our daughter Christina, who was twelve at the time and standing to his right, and asked, "Sweetheart, did you feel the power of the Lord flow out of my hand into yours?"

Time stood still. What would she say? A myriad of thoughts filled my mind in a millisecond. *This is Oral Roberts, for heaven's sake! Maybe I should tell him the power arced and reached me! After all, I was moved to tears!* I thanked the Lord that our youngest daughter, Sandy, was not there, for God only knows what she would have said. *O Lord, please intervene!* I thought.

Christina looked at me, she looked at her father, and then she looked directly at Brother Roberts and answered, "No, sir."

I held my breath and dared not look at anyone but my daughter, who needed the reassurance from me that all was good. I smiled at her to signal all was well. But what about Brother Roberts?

Being the man of God he is, he bent down and put his arms around our Tina and hugged her tightly, kissing her on the forehead. He told her that she was a brave girl to tell the truth and that he loved her for it.

She saw the Spirit of the Lord coming from him. I released the air from my lungs and repented of my fear. Christina was happy.

Happy are those who tell the truth and maintain purity in their hearts, for they shall see God!

7. Happy are the peacemakers.

We all want peace, but few of us are willing to do what is necessary to bring peace to the nations of the world or the world around us. When Christ was born, the angel declared to the frightened shepherds, "Glory to God in the highest, and on earth peace to people of good will." (See Luke 2:14.)

Yet the world has seen very few years of peace since Christ our Prince of Peace came. There is a story of a conversation between a dove and a sparrow. "Tell me the weight of a snowflake," a sparrow asked a wild dove.

"Nothing more than nothing," was the answer.

"In that case, I must tell you a marvelous story," the sparrow said. "I sat on the branch of a fir, close to its trunk, when it began to snow—not heavily, not in a raging blizzard—no, just like a dream, without a sound, and without any violence. Since I did not have anything better to do, I counted the snowflakes settling on the twigs and needles of my branch. Their number was exactly 3,742,952. When the 3,742,953rd flake dropped onto the branch, the branch broke off the tree."

Having said that, the sparrow flew away. The dove, since Noah's time an authority on the matter, thought about the story for a while and finally said to herself, "Perhaps only one person's voice is lacking for peace to come to the world."[9]

Perhaps only one voice is lacking for peace in your household. Perhaps only one voice is lacking for peace within your heart. Perhaps that voice is yours.

8. Happy are the persecuted for doing right.

The first four rules of happiness deal with what God wants to do in us. The next three reveal what comes out of us because of what God has done within us. The next two deal with how the world responds to us. Cyprian, a third-century martyr, wrote this powerful letter to his friend Donatus.

> This is a cheerful world as I see it from my garden under the shadows of my vines. But if I were to ascend some high mountain and look out over the wide lands, you know very well what I should see: brigands on the highways, pirates on the sea, armies fighting, cities burning; in the amphitheaters, men murdered to please applauding crowds; selfishness and cruelty and misery and despair under all roofs. It is a bad world, Donatus, an incredibly bad world. But I have discovered in the midst of it a quiet and holy people who have learned a great secret. They are despised and persecuted, but they care not. They are master of their souls. They have overcome the world. These people, Donatus, are the Christians—and I am one of them.[10]

Cyprian lived in a day when being persecuted for doing right was almost an art form! Yet today, good people are still being persecuted for doing right—sometimes even in a marriage relationship. This beatitude tells us that "happy are the persecuted for doing right." Our reward, our happiness for doing right, does not come from external circumstances—it comes from within. It is because of what God has done within us that we can maintain our joy even when others respond to us with some form of persecution.

> These things I have spoken to you, that My joy may remain in you, and that your joy may be full.
>
> —JOHN 15:11

9. Happy are the criticized.

The Lord is very clear about how we should respond to those who speak ill of us:

> But I tell you, Love your enemies and pray for those who persecute you, to show that you are the children of your Father Who is in heaven; for He makes His sun rise on the wicked and on the good, and makes the rain fall upon the upright and the wrongdoers [alike].
>
> —MATTHEW 5:44–45, AMP

We are to bless those who curse us.

What do we do when criticisms are true?

My husband describes the difference between *constructive criticism* and *destructive criticism* very clearly. Constructive criticism takes place when you criticize an individual, but when another person criticizes you, then that is destructive criticism.

Jamie Buckingham was a good friend of ours. His honesty and candor were so refreshing you could listen to him for hours. One day my husband and I were in his home visiting with him and his wife, Jackie, a sweet and precious partner to his dynamic ministry.

One of the many books Jamie wrote was *Daughter of Destiny*, a biographical account of the life of Kathryn Kuhlman. After listening to several stories about her ministry, I asked Jamie if he knew why she always wore her long signature dress with the flowing sleeves.

> **HE SAYS . . .**
>
> **Your attitude is never content until it's expressed. It determines your success or your failure.**

He told me that one day she received a letter from a gentleman who was very gracious and kind about his comments regarding her television program. However, he did have one criticism. He told her he was distracted by her constant pulling at her dress to maintain it below her knees. He suggested she wear a long dress.

Kathryn, who was very sensitive to criticism, read the letter and acknowledged that he was right. She wore long dresses from that day forward.

Jamie later wrote an article about her response:

> A lesser person would have responded with anger, or passed it off as just another senseless remark. But she was not that sort of lesser person. She heard. She coped. She let it help her toward her goal of communicating. All of which was possible because there was no root of bitterness to give a bad taste to everything that came into her life, which presented another viewpoint.[11]

Norman Vincent Peale once said, "The trouble with most of us is that we would rather be ruined by praise than saved by criticism."[12]

Our attitude is everything. A man who has a healthy attitude about himself will do exactly what the Bible says. He will bless his enemies when they attack him and will listen to his conscience and discern when he should change his path. As a result, this man will experience the kingdom of heaven.

The man who blesses his enemies and discerns when he must change will be a person who is happy with himself and happy with the world around him. Ultimately he will reflect the God who lives within him.

HINTS FOR HIM

True laughter is an outward expression of the joy that lies within. Strive for happiness in your life.

HINT: You can't become a comedian when you aren't one. So don't try.

HINT: Don't use your wife as the brunt of your jokes. It won't honor her, and God will not honor you!

HINT: Learn to laugh at yourself. Sometimes you are the greatest source of humor you will find.

HINT: Allow laughter to diffuse anger.

Pastor Hagee and I are blessed with a wonderful church family. Over the course of thirty-eight years of pastoring, we can honestly say that many people have blessed us...some by staying in our church and some by leaving. If you are a pastor or a pastor's wife, you know exactly what I'm talking about.

One day a former church member said something very cruel about our congregation. He was making it known that the reason he left our church was due to its ethnic makeup. My husband became incensed and was determined to "set the record straight" with this wayward soul. He went into his study and began to respond to the insulting remarks in the form of a letter.

There was a challenge, however. There is always a challenge to almost every situation in the ministry. I believe the Lord tosses them in to make sure we stay close to Him and His instruction.

The challenge: the author of the offensive remarks happened to be related to very loyal and precious church members. I reminded my husband of this very important fact, but no matter, his "hot button" had been pressed and there was no turning back. I followed him into the study and began to give him all the reasons why this letter of rebuke should not be written—all to no avail.

"John, the Word says to forgive as you have been forgiven!" I said as I quickly tried to remember scriptures to support my stand.

"I have forgiven them! But I have not forgotten what they said about the righteous!" he irritatingly responded.

"Remember that you are to bless your enemies!" I shouted.

"They don't deserve a blessing!" he shouted back, continuing to type as fast as his fingers could hit the keyboard—and hitting the keyboard they were.

I began to read over his shoulder and hyperventilate at the same time. I am the diplomat of the marriage. Pastor is known as the "tell-it-like-it-is" pastor, and I am known as the "what-he-really-meant-to-say-was..." pastor's wife.

I knew that this letter could not be sent; it would hurt too many people. But my husband was determined. He is a true shepherd to the sheep God has entrusted us with, and in his eyes, a great transgression has been committed when anyone hurts his church members.

The more I read the rebuke, the more I railed, "No! You can't say that!"

"Watch me!" was his heated response.

"You must show mercy!" I pleaded.

"They have been shown mercy; God would have given them leprosy!" he firmly retorted without taking his concentration from the keyboard.

I could see I wasn't getting through to him, and I became desperate. Suddenly, as if someone else was in control of my body, I did something I had never done before. I walked from behind him and stood by his computer keyboard as I pounded on the keyboard with all ten fingers as fast and as hard as I could.

The computer screen abruptly began to blink and groan as icons began appearing everywhere. Question marks, pound signs, asterisks, and exclamation marks took the place of the words of chastisement and reprimand. It was a surreal, out-of-body experience.

My husband tried to retrieve his document of hot coals, but he could not. He stared at the screen as if in a stupor and then looked over at me. The look he gave me was not a good one. I stared at him, and then my glazed gaze went back to the computer screen filled with electronic gibberish.

Silence filled the room as if a vacuum had sucked all the sound waves out of the air. I could not believe what I had done.

Then, what seemed to be eternal quiet was suddenly replaced by the two words that came from my husband's mouth. "You dimwit!" he shouted.

As if someone had snapped his fingers in front of my face, I was awakened from my trance as I heard his reaction to my exploit. I took my eyes from the screen, put my hands on my hips, and looked back at him with a "not-so-good look" as well. When you get a German and a Mexican mad at the same time, the battle lines are drawn, and sparks can really fly.

"I am not a dimwit!" I indignantly responded.

The stare-down was on. Neither one of us would retreat from our glares. Then suddenly, as unexpectedly as I had pounded on the keyboard, he began to laugh hysterically. I impulsively joined in. Before long we were both laughing so hard that tears were running down our faces, and we could hardly catch our breath.

I bent down and kissed his forehead as he stood to hug me. Once we stopped laughing and regained our composure, we agreed in prayer that the person making the remarks would be silenced by the Lord and that our congregation would be spared from hearing the evil comments that were meant for harm.

All was satisfied. The Lord had been called to intervene. Our church family would be covered by His protection. My husband released his frustrations on the keyboard of the computer. My diplomatic instincts were satisfied, and the letter of rebuke was lost in electronic eternity.

If we took the time to analyze the moments of anger and frustration toward our spouse, we would most likely find our annoyance was motivated by insignificant incidences that were overreacted to because of stress, anxiety, or something totally unrelated to our husband or wife. We must not leave the door open for the enemy to take our peace or our marriages through anger.

> "Be angry, and do not sin": do not let the sun down on your wrath, nor give place to the devil.
> —EPHESIANS 4:26–27

Allow laughter to defuse anger.

HINT: Be patient. Be patient in marriage; it will help you laugh with your wife when life isn't fair. Be patient with this world; it will give you a longer life.

My husband, by his own confession, is not a very patient man. I have been good for him. Time for me is a gift. I cherish it. I don't waste it, but I don't hurry through it, either. Two o'clock in the afternoon today will soon be two o'clock in the afternoon tomorrow; I simply enjoy the journey. My husband has had to endure my attitude about time and learn about patience.

One Sunday after church we took a plane to Houston to attend the wedding of the son of very dear friends of ours. It was a beautiful Jewish ceremony, and we were now waiting to enter the lavish reception. My husband was tired and couldn't understand why the reception was not underway an hour after the ceremony.

Some friends of ours were patiently waiting with us as my husband began to fidget. He kept looking at his watch and asking me why the doors to the reception room were not open. After I explained to him that it was not my wedding, he went to the men's room; he said he needed to kill time.

Concerned we would not be having a very pleasant evening, I went to those who were serving refreshments and asked them when they thought the reception would officially begin.

They gave me their *guesstimation*—one hour! I thought, *This is it. We are soon heading to the hotel for room service and an early night.* Our friend heard the answer and was amused to see how my husband would respond.

He came out of the men's room and asked if I had an update. "Yes," was my cautious answer.

"Well?" he asked.

"Soon." I responded.

"How soon?" he asked with a little more emphasis, yet cautious not to raise his voice among friends.

Our friends were curiously watching our exchange. "Very soon," I told him, aware that I was skating on thin ice.

Losing what was left of his frail patience, he firmly called my name. "Diana! How long before the reception begins?"

Our friend came to my rescue. "Well, Reverend Hagee, let me put it this way; in terms of eternity...not long."

With that we all burst out laughing and had a wonderful evening. Laughter can change everything. "How long must I be happy?" you might ask. In terms of eternity—forever.

From Dr. Anne

In the 1930s and 1940s there was a radio show called *Fibber McGee and Molly*. One line from Molly that worked its way into every episode was, "T'aint funny, McGee!" It came after Fibber laughed at something she had taken quite seriously. She had failed to share his humor.

Marriage can be a lot of fun—if you don't take it too seriously. Life is so much easier to manage when we see how ridiculous many problems in our lives really are. Humor can diffuse tension. When you are able to identify quickly and consistently an interaction that leads to a recurring argument between you and your spouse, you can prevent family disruption. You can even choose to use this knowledge to establish an inside joke, between you and your husband, that can alleviate the tension when this issue rears its head again. Many couples who have been married ten-plus years have one-liners that prompt a squeeze of the hand and a knowing smile.

Humor requires that two people see the same thing as *funny*. A one-sided joke is insensitive, cruel, and rude. There is a line between humor and humiliation that, if not sensitively recognized, can destroy confidence and trust. A compassionate spouse learns that line quickly and generalizes the information and skills to other situations. Having fun and sharing humorous experiences and thoughts can be like a mini-vacation offering relief to the seriousness of everyday life. Knowing the appropriate time, place, and subject requires wisdom and maturity. After a quarrel, a wife said to her husband, "You know, I was a fool when I married you."

The husband replied, "Yes, dear, but I was in love and didn't notice it."

Let God show you how your spouse can enrich your life, not reflect it. Your spouse is not a reflective image of yourself. You are a reflection of God, and so is he. Knowing when to make light of your differences is the way to grow. We are able to be different and still be safe. We don't have to feel abandoned and alone because we have differences.

Don't make light of marriage intimacy. Be sensitive to subjects your husband considers uncompromisingly serious. Be of one mind and one accord. A marriage without a sense of humor is like a pebble in your shoe that feels like a boulder the longer you walk on it. Laughter removes the pebble.

There isn't a lot that happens in life that doesn't have a light side. Even the serious things don't have to have serious lasting effects. Laughter's importance can be observed in tense situations. It can be used to defuse potentially explosive situations. Remembering is good. Learning is good. Not having to have scars from wounds is better. Properly applied, humor can deflate a tense argument. It gives you a different perspective.

Lighten up, and let your family breathe and develop a perspective that encourages humor. Tomorrow's memories are being made today. Let them be good ones. Smile quickly, and laugh a lot!

CLOSING PRAYERS

We are in this world, not of it. We are not rewarded for being able to live with one foot in the world and the other in the church. No, we are rewarded for being and doing right despite the outward conditions and pressures we face. This kind of happiness can only come directly from the throne of the living God.

PRAYER OF REPENTANCE

Father, I have needed to laugh for a long time. I have blamed my lack of joy on my husband. Forgive me. I have not looked inward. I must find my joy in You and within Your Word. I have also been entirely too serious in my dealings with my husband. I have refused to be derailed from my anger. My husband has tried to make peace with me by joking and letting me see how sorry he is for my upset. I have refused to let it go and "drop it," and I have carried the dis-agreement beyond the stopping place. I will be aware of this in the future and will be willing to sacrifice my need to be angry. Forgive me, Lord Jesus, for presenting a hostile atmosphere in my home. I have allowed fear and anger to take the place of Your joy and peace in my home. I repent and will make changes according to Your Word. Amen.

PRAYER OF NEW BEGINNINGS

Thank You, Lord, for my marriage, which brings me so much pleasure. You have told us that a merry heart does us good like a medicine. Thank You for taking our burdens and worries so we can see the lighter side of our lives. Thank You for laughter and joy. Your joy is truly my strength. I accept for my own life the promise that You gave to Job, promising to fill my mouth with laughter and my lips with joyful shouting. I will pass that blessing on to my family.

You have taken me from the bondage of negative issues and given me peace and resolution. I will learn to be happy in all things, for You are the source of my joy and my strength. With Your help, I can do anything. I love You, Jesus. Amen.

nine

Want Number Two:
ROMANCE

Set me as a seal upon your heart, as a seal upon your arm; for love is as strong as death.... Many waters cannot quench love, nor can the floods drown it.
—SONG OF SOLOMON 8:6–7

EVERY WEEK THE public is bombarded with magazines about the "beautiful people." You know the magazines—if you don't subscribe to them, you catch a glimpse of the covers as you wait to check out at the grocery counter. They contain pictures of half of the world's beautiful people dating the other half of the world's beautiful people. Each person is usually posed with someone of the opposite sex, holding hands or touching in one manner or another. If you read the cover stories, each will probably mention somewhere in the caption that this couple is "romantically involved."

But read a subsequent issue of the same magazine, and you will probably notice that something strange has happened: the two persons you saw linking arms in January are no longer linking arms in March. The caption informs you that January's couple has gone their separate ways, but March has brought a new "romantic interest." Buy next month's issue, and see what happens!

Is it *romance* or *infatuation*? Columnist Ann Landers made a very clear distinction between infatuation and romantic love: "Infatuation is instant desire—one set of glands calling to another. Love is friendship that has caught fire. It takes root and grows, one day at a time."[1]

Infatuation is marked by a feeling of insecurity. You are excited and eager, but not genuinely happy. There are nagging doubts, unanswered questions, little bits and pieces about your beloved that you would just as soon not examine too closely. It might spoil the dream.

Love is quiet understanding and the mature acceptance of imperfection. It is real. It gives you strength and grows beyond you—to bolster your beloved. You are warmed by his presence, even when he is away. Miles do not separate you. You want him nearer. But near or far, you know he is yours, and you can wait.

Infatuation says, "We must get married right away. I can't risk losing him."

Love says, "Be patient. Don't panic. Plan your future with confidence."

Infatuation has an element of sexual excitement. If you are honest, you will admit it is difficult to be in one another's company unless you are sure it will end in intimacy.

Love is the maturation of friendship. You must be friends before you can be lovers.

Infatuation lacks confidence. When he's away, you wonder if he's cheating. Sometimes you even check.

Love means trust. You are calm, secure, and unthreatened. He feels that trust, and it makes him even more trustworthy.

Infatuation might lead you to do things you'll regret later, but love never will. Love is an upper. To love makes you look up. It makes you think up. It makes you a better person than you were before. The woman who feels that way knows true love.

Seven Ways to Romance Your Husband

I must be honest. I purposefully did not read my husband's section of this book so I would not be influenced by its content. However, he and I together sat in our bedroom and created the following seven romantic things a man and a woman can do for one another to generate romance in their marriage.

There is a misconception that men want *only* sex and women want *only* romance. How untrue. This misinformation has contributed to more marriage problems than any of us care to acknowledge.

But before we take a look at the seven ways to romance your husband, please understand that romance is not sex. In all the research I

HE SAYS...

For some women, being romantic means buying her flowers....Whatever spells *romance* for your wife, all women respond to romance and want more of it.

did for this book, secular and Christian alike, the common thread was a clear distinction between *romantic love* and *sexual intimacy*.

Romance is so much more. Romance lasts. Romance generates a love so deep that if sex were not possible for whatever reason, love would still grow. Romantic affection creates the necessary environment for a good marriage, and sex is one of the main events. Romance is precious.

Consider these seven ways to romance *your* husband.

1. Tell him you love him.

> Tell me, O you whom my soul loves...
> —SONG OF SOLOMON 1:7, AMP

The old "I told you I loved you when I married you, and if I ever change my mind, I'll tell you" line is not applicable here. A man wants to hear these three little words come from your mouth and your heart often.

A phone call during the day with a simple "I love you" is great. Ladies, don't overdo—remember, quality vs. quantity; you don't want to smother the man!

Love notes in his briefcase, travel bag, or clothes drawer does wonders to confirm your love for him. Sign your note with a kiss, wearing his favorite color lipstick, and spray your perfume on it! An e-mail with a scripture of blessing over your husband, along with a P.S. that says "I love you," will bring a smile to his heart.

Men want to know they are loved.

2. Praise him.

> O my love, how beautiful you are! There is no flaw in you!
> —SONG OF SOLOMON 4:7, AMP

Encouragement is so important. To tell your husband you are proud of him does more for him than you know. A wife's support of her husband contributes more to his success than any other factor. As the Lord encourages His own, so should a wife encourage her husband and make him aware that she appreciates all he does for her and their family.

We live in an award-conscious society. Why not begin a tradition in your family and award your husband for the good things he has done? Why not ask your children to award their father on special occasions with the "Best Father" trophy, and let them explain why he has earned this prestigious award, before time takes its toll on all of us!

A man stopped at a flower shop to order some flowers to be wired to his mother, who lived two hundred miles away. As he got out of his car, he noticed a young girl sitting outside the flower shop crying. Concerned, he asked her what was wrong. She replied, "I wanted to buy a red rose for my mother, but I only have a dollar, and a rose costs three dollars."

The man, warmed by her desire to bless her mother, said, "Come with me. I'll buy you a rose." The little girl gratefully smiled. The man bought the single rose for the girl and ordered the flowers for his own mother.

As they were leaving the shop, he offered the young girl a ride home. Excited, she responded, "Yes, please! You can take me to my mother!" She directed him to the local cemetery where she lovingly placed the rose on her mother's freshly dug grave.

The man returned to the flower shop, canceled the order, picked up a bouquet of a dozen red roses, and drove the two hundred miles to his mother's home where he presented the flowers in person.[2]

Men want to know they are important; don't take them for granted.

3. Prepare a special meal for him.

> Sustain me with raisins, refresh me with apples, for I am sick with love.
> —Song of Solomon 2:5, amp

Yes, I really did write that. No, I wasn't forced. When a man offers to take his wife out to dinner, it is a very, very nice gesture that shows she is greatly appreciated. She doesn't have to spend hours in the kitchen cooking and cleaning. She is blessed and feels special.

When she prepares a special meal for her husband, he is aware of the time she put forth in creating it. She has let him know he is important enough to her that she is willing to sacrifice her time and effort to make this loving gesture.

A woman who hated to cook told her homemaking girlfriend that the quickest way to a man's heart was not his stomach; it was his chest![3] If you don't like to cook, it is even more of a romantic signal to prepare a special meal for him because he knows you are going out of your way to please him.

I love to cook, so I must make this kind of romance a little unique. When my husband comes home in the evening, he walks into the kitchen, gives me a hug and a kiss, and asks how my day went. Then he goes into his study and drops off his briefcase, which is filled with research for Sunday's sermon or the latest book he is writing. From there he goes into our bedroom and watches the evening news until dinner is ready.

If, when he comes through the door, I tell him that he can't go into our bedroom because I have something special planned, he immediately smiles and usually says, "Aw," no matter how tough the day has been. The mood has been set.

When I call him to dinner, he walks into our bedroom with anticipation and sees a small table set with linen and china in front of the fireplace. There are candles on the table and a single red rose in a crystal vase. He loves red. The only light in the room comes from the lit candles and the fire. I then serve a five-course dinner.

Men like to be pampered.

4. Give him gifts.

> The mandrakes give forth fragrance, and over our doors are all manner of choice fruits, new and old, which I have laid up for you, O my beloved!
> —SONG OF SOLOMON 7:13, AMP

How do you feel when your husband buys a present for you? You feel like a queen with all the wealth of the world. Give gifts to your husband, too. The gift doesn't have to be expensive. The fact that you thought of it with him in mind will be more than sufficient.

I give my husband ties. He loves bold, red ties. Sometimes I frame a special picture of the two of us, or one of him with the children or grandbabies. Think of what would especially bless your husband, *and do it*.

Men love presents.

5. Surprise him.

> Arise, my darling, my beautiful one, and come with me.
> —SONG OF SOLOMON 2:10, NIV

This could be dangerous. The biggest surprise I ever gave my husband was given one Sunday evening during church services twenty-four years ago.

I had something very important to tell him, and he was busy preparing for the evening service and did not want me to bother him. I kept trying to interrupt him in my usual persistent manner, and he kept putting me off: "Just another minute." Time came for service, and he looked up and asked what I needed. I told him it could wait for church to be over.

Well, by now you probably know me—I couldn't stand it, so I wrote a note, folded it in two, and asked an usher to take the note to my husband on the platform during the music portion of our service. John took the piece of paper and opened it. His eyes opened wide, and he made the thumbs-up sign and flashed a big smile my way. What did the note say? It was my announcement to him that we were going to have a baby!

No, you don't have to get pregnant to surprise your husband! There are so many ways to create romance with surprises. My sister surprises her husband with bed-and-breakfast weekends. What about a picnic?

Date nights make for great surprises! Occasionally I call my husband and ask him if he would like to have an exciting date for the evening. I make arrangements for dinner and a movie. (It's always nice to be treated, so make sure the evening is paid for.)

Sometimes I put his favorite chocolate on his pillow so he can find it when he prepares for bed. The anticipation that surprises create is so essential for romance. Men love surprises.

6. The power of your touch

> Let him kiss me with the kisses of his mouth!...For your love is better than wine!
> —SONG OF SOLOMON 1:2, AMP

One of my friends dated a man who never showed her affection when they were out together. I once asked her about it, and she said he did not like to display a "public show of affection." I remember thinking to myself, *I don't believe him.* They eventually broke up, and she married a wonderful young man who believes in holding hands and hugging. They are very happy.

A couple of years later, I saw her former boyfriend with his new girl-friend at a restaurant. I smiled as I saw him affectionately hold the hand of the woman he loved. True romantic love needs an affectionate touch to survive.

> **HE SAYS...**
>
> **When a wife says "Come and hold me" to her husband, he rubs his hands together as his testosterone meter explodes and responds, "All right..." He is ready for raw sex. She simply wants affection.**

It is very important to show affection to your husband every opportunity you get. Take his hand when you are walking together, or pat his shoulder as you pass by him. Kiss him often. Even if it hasn't been part of your past behavior, try beginning anew by giving him what it is you want in return.

One of the most beautiful pictures of romance I have ever seen is one I witness every Sunday morning at Cornerstone Church. On the front row center of the second section sit a wonderful man and his precious wife. They are in their late eighties. They sit so close to each other you couldn't get a sheet of paper between them. Every Sunday they hold each other's hand. These two wrinkled and gnarled hands are clasped tightly, and the other two hands are raised in praise and worship to the Lord.

What a statement they make! The message of romance they send every Sunday is a memorial to the love they have for each other and the love they have for God.

Men love hugs and kisses.

7. Loyalty

I am my beloved's...and my beloved is mine!
—SONG OF SOLOMON 6:3, AMP

I was a little taken by surprise when my husband told me that one of the romantic things about our relationship to him was my loyalty. He said that as a man, there is nothing so special as to know that the woman you love can be trusted and that she will never bring you heartache.

Proverbs 31 describes the perfect woman as being one in whom "her husband safely trusts" (v. 11). Trust is the fabric of every human connection. Without trust there can be no confidence, emotional stability, or hope for the future. Trust is the cornerstone of your marriage relationship.

Remember the sacred vows you made. They are your word and your bond. To know that my Lord made a vow to me at the cross when I repented before Him and received Him as my Savior, and that vow will never be broken, gives me a peace and a comfort that cannot be duplicated.

> **HE SAYS . . .**
> **May I ask you this question? Is your love loyal?**

Because of the faith I have in a God who never fails, I want to please Him even more. I want Him to know that I will never turn away and serve another god. I may disappoint Him from time to time, but I am His and will never abandon my faith in Him.

HINTS FOR HIM

This is simple. Every "romance rule" I gave to women in this chapter, I equally give to the husband as a "ditto romance rule" for keeping his marriage a fertile ground for romance. To me the most romantic relationships I have ever seen are not the young newlyweds who hopelessly cling to each other, or the new parents who hold the product of their love in their arms. No, the most romantic relationships are between couples who have been married thirty, forty, fifty, sixty years—they know the secret to true romance.

FROM DR. ANNE

An excellent marriage takes effort. You probably liked your husband the first time you met him. You began to enjoy spending time together. You began to understand each other's family history. Over the years, you shared experiences and developed your own history together. Affection grew with the passage of time.

Sometimes we let those romantic feelings grow cool over time. Are you still giving your time to shared experiences and continuing to develop the history that stimulates affection and appreciation?

Our understanding of the relationship God has with His children is a direct correlation to our understanding of the marriage relationship. Without that spiritual understanding, we have absolutely no concept of the sacrifice that is necessary to allow marriage to meet the needs of the two individuals involved and to meet the standards set by God Almighty. In the most challenging times of our lives, God cares for us, comforts us, and reveals His love to us.

In the same way, a woman wants, and needs, to feel the care and comfort of her husband's life. She wants to feel "special" to him. She holds a place in the life of her husband that can't be met by anyone or anything except her. When she walks into the room he lights up. He values her personality. He likes the way she laughs, the way she smiles, the way she presents herself. He understands her when no one else seems to; he forgives her imperfections.

How fabulous to not have to be perfect to be loved! How wonderful to know that when your husband places a gentle hand over yours that you are being reassured of your value.

Wives, don't ever forget that you get what you give. You will be accepted, appreciated, and affectionately acknowledged as you are genuinely willing to accept, appreciate, and acknowledge your husband. Maturity, history, and sharing should increase the love and affection that you have for your husband and that he has for you. Couples who are able to reflect the attributes of trustworthiness and commitment are more able to abandon themselves to a sensual marriage experience. First Corinthians 13:7 reminds us that love is to show no end of its trust.

I believe that we get what we give. I believe in the law of reciprocity as it pertains to relationships. It is no coincidence that mathematics—the language of science—encodes logic into a device called an *equation*, which requires its elements to be equivalent on opposite sides of the argument.

Sir Isaac Newton captured the essence of natural balance when he codified the law of physics, which states that every action precipitates an equal and opposite reaction. Cause and effect: for every up there is a down; you get what you give eventually.

If you want your husband to be "Mr. Right," then you must first see that you are "Mrs. Right." We must each take responsibility for ourselves as well as for the relationship.

Our God loved us when we were yet unlovable, but don't be so foolish as to expect that from your husband. God is God; human beings are human beings, although we are striving to be more God-like. My prayer for you is that God will develop in you the softness and sweetness that He created you to have. May your husband receive the loving affection that you show to him and return it in an overflowing proportion.

Allow the qualities you want in your husband to be found in your own life.

CLOSING PRAYERS

To tell your husband often that you love him—*essential*. To praise him for his accomplishments—*uplifting*. When you prepare a candlelight dinner for him—*romantic*. Surprising him with a special evening—*intimate*. To leave loving notes for him to find—*heartwarming*. Giving him hugs and kisses—*affectionate*. And being loyal to him **always**—*priceless*.

PRAYER OF REPENTANCE

Lord, I have failed to show my husband the spontaneous affection and appreciation that he really needs. I am sometimes too caught up in my own world of job, children, church, and personal desires, and I have nothing left for my husband. I have been wrong. I have failed to tell him that I love him. I have not tried to uplift him with praise, but I am quick to criticize. I am so busy that I seldom show him I care by preparing a special meal or giving him a small gift as a token of my love for him. I can't remember the last time I surprised him. He needs my romantic attention, and I have failed to give it. I don't provide loving pats or kisses because I fear rejection or am too preoccupied with my own life. I have been disloyal to him, and I need Your forgiveness—and his—to begin anew in my marriage. Forgive me, Lord, for breaking my vows to You and to my husband. I may be loyal to him, but I don't give him much evidence of that loyalty in my actions. I need to confirm my loyalty to him and let him know that he is the only man I want or need. I desire a new marriage, Lord, one that will fulfill both my husband's and my needs and desires. I have not given of myself, yet I have demanded to receive. I ask for Your forgiveness and for Your strength to try again and to succeed. Amen.

PRAYER OF NEW BEGINNINGS

Lord, I truly want to begin over. I want to be romantically attracted to my husband as I was when our relationship was fresh and exciting. I want him to be attracted to me in the same way. I pray that I will learn to be aware of how I respond to his needs and desires and that I can communicate mine to him. I ask for You to help me to develop an immediate response of love and respect instead of fear and rejection. I will give to my husband as You have given to me. You have been generous with Your grace and mercy toward me and have loved me when I have been unlovable. Thank You, Father. Please help me make my marriage a thing of love, romance, and loyalty. I want us to be one of those couples who hold hands and give hugs and kisses to each other when we are old and gray. I want to keep my sacred covenant to You and to my husband. I want to make him happy that he is married to me. I need Your help, Lord, and I know I will receive it, for You are faithful. I love You. Amen.

GODLY MAN

ten

> For the grace of God that brings salvation has
> appeared to all men. It teaches us to say "No" to
> ungodliness and worldly passions, and to live self-
> controlled, upright and godly lives in this present
> age, while we wait for the blessed hope—the glorious
> appearing of our great God and Savior, Jesus Christ,
> who gave himself for us to redeem us from all
> wickedness and to purify for himself a people that
> are his very own, eager to do what is good.
> —TITUS 2:11–14, NIV

S O YOU WANT a godly man? Perhaps the first question should be, "Do you know how to recognize a godly man?" In essence, the characteristics that the women in our church have listed as their ten "wants" in a man are the characteristics of a godly man. We have discussed those characteristics in this book.

THE BIBLE'S GODLY MEN

When I read these top ten *wants,* from the least to the most desired, I immediately began to think of some of the heroes of the Bible, the men in Scripture whom we identify as truly godly men. Have you ever wondered what it might be like to be married to one of them?

Noah

Think of Noah…the Scriptures say he was a "just and righteous man, blameless in his [evil] generation; Noah walked [in habitual fellowship] with God" (Gen. 6:9, AMP). God knew Noah to be a godly man. Now, go into the theater of the mind for a moment with me, and imagine what it would be like to be married to Noah.

He comes home one afternoon with architectural plans in his hands and tells you he has had a visitation from the Lord Himself. The great I AM has commanded him to do something he has never done before—with no budget and no true understanding of its purpose. Furthermore, God is going to destroy the earth with water from the skies—a phenomenon not witnessed by any human being. So, he quits his job and begins his assignment.

Then he tells you that after his building project is completed, you and he and the children will take a long cruise. However, he doesn't know exactly *where* or for *how long*. And there is one more catch—your part! You must help him gather and care for those who will travel with your family, something about "two by two." You will have a thankless job, but he feels very strongly that he should obey the wishes of the Lord, for Jehovah God has promised to provide.

Would you willingly work by his side?

Abraham

Abraham was commanded by God to leave a very comfortable home and to depart from his family and his country. God loves Abraham so much that He promises Abraham to give him a seven-clause covenant. (See Genesis 17:1–8.)

1. I will make you a great nation.
2. I will bless you.
3. I will make your name great.
4. You shall be a blessing.
5. I will bless those who bless you.
6. I will curse those who curse you.
7. In you, all the families of the earth shall be blessed.

This man has surely found favor with the Lord. What kind of a husband would he make?

Let's examine Abraham a bit further. He comes to you and recounts his visit with God, and he tells you that he doesn't really know where the two of you will be going. However, you must leave the dream house you just built and travel in a caravan. Finally, he persuades you to leave your lavish lifestyle and all that is important to you. He also assures you that Yahweh has promised to bless him with descendents *that will be too many to count*.

Oh, and it gets better, sweetheart! While on your trip to "God only knows where," Abraham convinces you to act *as his sister* for *his* protection. This hurts your feelings, and you feel rejected. Even though this request from Abraham will put *you* in imminent danger, you think about it a bit. Still hurt, you finally agree.

Time passes, and the journey, which has been tough, finds you older now. You have given this man some of the best years of your life. You have a weak moment (all women are allowed their fair measure of weak moments). You determine that at your present age, you probably won't produce an heir for your husband. Therefore, you suggest—only once, I might add—that he go into your handmaiden and produce a child with her. Without hesitation he agrees, *a little too quickly, if you ask me*. To add insult to injury, your favorite handmaiden, now heavy with your husband's child, is flaunting her favored status.

Would you leave your home and go with this man?

Moses

Moses was a man so loved of God that God chose him to lead His people, the apple of His eye, out of bondage. Moses is the man whom God trusted with His law. What would it be like married to Moses? Moses is gone days at a time on spiritual mountain retreats without you. When he is home, he is overwhelmed with his task of leading millions of people *somewhere,* to arrive *sometime.* It seems to you that you are hopelessly stuck in the desert. Moses spends all his daylight hours—and well into the night—in counseling sessions trying to solve the chosen people's problems.

He brings their problems home with him every night. You become so upset that you call your father to take Moses to lunch so he can advise him on how to lessen his workload. The marriage is stressed. When will it end—this endless desert wandering with these complaining travel companions who demand all of your husband's time?

Would you support this man and his ministry?

David

David was a man after God's own heart, a leader among men, a great warrior—and an adulterer and a murderer and a failure as a father. What would it have been like to be married to him?

HE SAYS...

The sooner you recognize your imperfection and the fact that you are, on your best day, a fatally flawed mortal, living day-to-day by the grace of God, the sooner you will be happy.

All these men have something in common. *They were flawed individuals chosen by a flawless God to do His will.* In order to accomplish their purposes, these men had to have a very supportive and godly woman by their side.

Today, we too are like these men—we are all flawed creatures. But there is a remarkable difference: the blood of a faultless Lamb covers us. These men lived under the Law; we live under the grace and mercy of our Savior Jesus Christ. It is His mercy that keeps us from getting what we deserve and His grace that gives us what we do not deserve.

CAN MY HUSBAND BECOME A GODLY MAN?

The question remains. What is a godly man, and how can you help your husband to become one?

A godly man is a reflection of his Savior. He must have the mind of God. He must see what God sees. He must have the heart of God. He must be the hand of God.

Booker T. Washington, in his autobiography *Up From Slavery,* told of a beautiful incident demonstrating his older brother's love. He said that the shirts worn on his plantation by the slaves were made of a tough, bristly, crude flax fiber. As a young boy, the garment was so abrasive to his tender, sensitive skin that it caused him a great deal of pain and discomfort. His older brother, moved by his brother's suffering, would wear Booker's new shirts until they were broken in and smoother to the touch. He would allow his own skin to become raw with irritation. Booker said it was one of the most profound acts of kindness he ever experienced.[1]

We do not know the older brother's name, but we can recognize the spirit that motivated him as Christ's. You may not remember a godly man's name, but you will never forget the name of the God he serves.

Another example of a godly man comes from the story of a godly Salvation Army missionary. Tears glistened in the eyes of the Salvation Army officer as he looked at the three men before him. Dr. Shaw was a medical missionary who had just arrived in India, where he had been assigned to a leper colony. Before him he saw three men who had iron clasps around their hands and feet, which were cutting into their infected, diseased flesh. Led by compassion, the doctor asked the guard to release the men. The guards protested, telling the doctor that they were not only lepers, but criminals as well.

"I'll be responsible," the doctor said. "They are suffering enough already." He asked for the keys, then knelt and tenderly removed the shackles and treated their open sores.

About two weeks later the doctor had second thoughts about freeing the criminals. It was necessary for him to make an overnight trip—and he had to leave his wife and child alone. His wife insisted that she was not afraid, for God would be with them. With that assurance, the doctor left on his journey.

The next morning the doctor's wife went to the door of her home to find the three men lying on her front steps. One of the men explained to the startled woman, "We know the doctor go. We stay here all night so no harm come to you."[2] These dangerous men responded to the act of love so mercifully given by the kind doctor.

THE MIND OF HIS FATHER

A godly man has the mind of his Father when he sees the hurting and those bound by the ravages of sin. He thinks as God thinks, in terms of love and compassion for the loveless.

One father always ended grace over the family meal with these words: "Come, Lord Jesus, be our guest, and bless what You have provided." One day his little son asked him a very important question.

"Papa, every evening you ask Jesus to come and be our guest, but He never comes."

"My son," replied the father, "we can only wait. But we know that He will not refuse our invitation."

"Well, then," asked the little boy, "if we invite Him to come and have dinner with us, why don't we set a place for Him at the table?" Moved by his son's innocence, the father allowed the boy to set a place at the table for Jesus.

Suddenly, they heard a knock at the door. When they opened it, a poor, helpless, little orphan stood shivering in the cold. The son looked at the hungry young child in the doorway for a moment, and he turned to his father and said, "I see Jesus couldn't come today, so He sent this boy in His place."

The father said little as his son brought the orphan to the table and sat him at the place reserved for Christ. A godly man must see the world and those around him through the eyes of God.[3]

On one of our many trips to Israel, Pastor Hagee and I were privileged to see one of the most beautiful acts of the heart. While on the flight to the Holy Land, two of the ministry partners with whom we were traveling shared their testimony with Pastor and me.

They had accepted Christ while watching my husband present one of his sermons through television. They told of the homosexual lifestyle they turned away from and the newfound joy that was now theirs. Thrilled with their new life, they were now on the trip of a lifetime.

Sadly, because of their past lifestyle, one of them was suffering from AIDS and was concerned what others on the trip might think. My husband assured them that all would be fine and that they should not be concerned with anything other than enjoying the life-changing journey they were about to experience.

One evening soon after our arrival, while in Tiberius we decided to take a walk after dinner. The young man who was ill was quite weak and frail after the long plane ride and could hardly walk. We provided a wheelchair for him. After much prayer, the young man gave my husband permission to tell the others in our group that he was ill and needed their prayers and assistance.

I remember my husband's prayers that evening as we held hands and asked the Lord to prepare the group for the news regarding our young friend. "Father, give them Your ears as they hear this news, and keep them from fear as they respond to this child of God with Your loving heart."

The next morning during our time of devotion, we told the group of our young friend's need for healing from this dreaded disease. With tears in their eyes, members of the group came up to him one by one and knelt around him as, together, we agreed in prayer for his healing.

From that moment on, the men of the tour would take turns pushing the young man's wheelchair and helping him on and off the bus. We saw them laugh with him and sit with him at meals and share each other's lives. It was a wonderful testimony of God's love.

But the most profound moment for me took place at the Garden Tomb. We had our time of praise and worship where we shared the

Lord's communion with one another, then released the people to enter into the empty tomb. One by one they entered in. One by one they came out in tears as they left the barren, hollowed-out cave.

My husband and I were standing on the upper platform watching these precious pilgrims experience a very solemn moment, when something beautiful happened. The young man was sitting in his chair several yards from the tomb, because the large stones of the Garden made it difficult to maneuver his wheelchair. Two of the men from our group came to him and placed their arms under his body as he anchored his frail arms around their shoulders. These men, never once concerned for their own health, carried their brother toward the tomb.

The people who were gathered around the doorway made a path for the three men to enter the dark mausoleum. All was quiet. All bowed their heads and prayed. The three men walked out of the tomb with tears flowing down their faces.

My husband and I joined in their tears. We felt privileged to be able to see a demonstration of the heart of the living God arising out of that empty tomb.

A small orphaned boy lived with his grandmother. One night their house caught fire. The grandmother, trying to rescue the little boy asleep upstairs, perished in the smoke and flames. A crowd gathered around the burning house. The boy's cries for help were heard above the crackling of the vicious blaze. No one seemed to know what to do, for the front of the house was a mass of flames.

Suddenly, a stranger rushed from the crowd and circled to the back. He spotted an iron pipe that reached to an upstairs window. He disappeared for a minute, and then reappeared with the boy in his arms. Amid the cheers of the crowd, he climbed down the hot pipe as the boy hung around his neck.

> **HE SAYS . . .**
>
> **Do you want to do something great for God? Be kind to His children! Kindness is a language that the deaf can hear and the blind can see.**

Weeks later, a public hearing was held in the town hall to determine in whose custody the boy would be placed. Each person who wanted the boy was allowed to speak briefly. The first man said, "I have a big farm, and everybody needs the out of doors."

The second man told of the advantages he could provide. "I'm a teacher. I have a large library. The boy would get a good education."

Others spoke. Finally the richest man in the community said, "I'm wealthy, and I could give the boy everything mentioned tonight—a farm, an education, and even more, including money and travel. I'd like him in my home."

The chairman asked if anyone else wanted to say a word. From the back rose a stranger who had slipped in unnoticed. As he walked to the front of the room, deep suffering showed on his face. Slowly the stranger removed his hands from his pockets.

A gasp went up from the crowd. The little boy, whose eyes had been focused on the ground until now, looked up. The man's hands were terribly scarred. Suddenly, looking into the man's face, the boy cried out in recognition. Here was the man who had saved his life. His hands had been scarred from climbing up and down the hot pipe as he salvaged the child from certain death.

With a leap the boy threw himself around the stranger's neck and once more held on for life. The farmer rose and left. The teacher, too. Then the rich man. Everyone departed, leaving the boy in the scarred hands of the man who had won him without a word.

> **HE SAYS . . .**
>
> **Remember: God has no superstars! He only has servants. Servants are willing to be poured out in an endless stream of the love of God.**

The godly man sees the scarred hands of his Savior when reaching out with his own hands to his wife, his children, or to a stranger in good deeds and kindness.

And finally a godly man must learn to say *no* to the world. The world does not recognize the righteousness of the God whom we serve. The world charms its victims with the "feel good" philosophy of our day. The world teaches that there is no right or wrong; it's all *relative*. The world entices with pleasure and rejects self-sacrifice.

The Word of God says that the man who says *no* to the world and *yes* to God is happy, fortunate, and to be envied because he fears, reveres, and worships the Lord. A godly man will walk in the path that God has set before him according to the commandments He has given.

HINTS FOR HIM

A godly man is:

1. Faithful
2. A spiritual leader
3. Respectful
4. A family man
5. A provider
6. Honest
7. A good communicator
8. Happy
9. Loving

FROM DR. ANNE

Women often *think* they know what they want, but, by nature, they are unwilling to allow God to develop in man the qualities and attributes that will ultimately result in God's giving them a man who is the true desire of their heart.

The top ten characteristics from the survey in this book result in obtaining a woman's number one desire, which is for a godly man. Yet all ten are contingent upon the woman allowing God to take over.

So often, manipulation of a man through circumstances and decisions is labeled *cute, funny*, or *a perfect way for a woman to get her way and fool the man into believing the idea was his*. God says that this is witchcraft. Manipulation and control are Satan's way of inserting himself into the relationship.

As women, we are only in charge to the extent that we are submitted to God's perfect will through His Word. Our minds require a renewing and washing with the Word through the direction of the Holy Spirit. How can we as women not thwart or stop God from developing in our husbands the qualities that will answer our prayers? How can we be helpmates to God in the process?

God gave to each of us His own Spirit to guide, build, counsel, and teach. He gives wisdom, understanding, good judgment, and strength. He ministers truth, reprimands, and gives counsel for correction.

There is absolutely NO passage in the Bible where women are given the mandate or authority to take on the Holy Spirit's role. You are to be only what God requires of you. Becoming your husband's *Holy Spirit* is not a requirement—indeed, it is blasphemy for you to assume that role.

CLOSING PRAYERS

As you pray for a godly man to come into your life, remember that a godly man deserves a godly wife. You must learn to humbly submit yourself in marriage to a godly man and to have a fervent commitment to the Lord as you nurture the next generation. You must learn to hear the voice of God and to take the path He has charted for you to become all you can be. He will give you all that you have desired to have. Live according to His plan, which will bring you blessings untold and a *soul satisfaction* that will be incomparable to anything else.

PRAYER OF REPENTANCE

O Lord, I have allowed myself to be more influenced by the roles that society has laid out for me than by Your infallible, inspired Word. Please forgive me. I am a good woman, Lord. I don't set out intentionally to counter Your will. I become distracted and influenced by the things of this world, not by Your guidance. Help me, Lord God, please. I am asking for a renewed mind so that You can teach me Your ways and precepts. I repent and will make an active effort to please You. I will strive to be the godly woman my husband needs so that he can become the godly man You intended him to be.

PRAYER OF NEW BEGINNINGS

Thank You, Father, for Your love, which gives me and my family another chance to get things right. I will not raise my children or conduct myself as a person of the world, but as a child of God. Help me, Lord God, to say no to this world and yes to You.

I know that You are faithful and will make my family a reflection of Your very best. As a wife and mother, I have been blessed by You with the opportunity to love and be loved. I will show my love by actively honoring my husband and allowing him to be the head of our household and the priest You have placed over us. I give You praise, honor, and glory for Your goodness and continued blessings. Thank You, Father, for new beginnings.

eleven

THE TORAH WAY

Thus says the Lord: Let not the wise and skillful
person glory and boast in his wisdom and skill; let
not the mighty and powerful person glory and boast
in his strength and power; let not the person who
is rich [in physical gratification and earthly wealth]
glory and boast in his [temporal satisfactions and
earthly] riches; but let him who glories glory in this:
that he understands and knows Me [personally and
practically, directly discerning and recognizing
My character], that I am the Lord, Who practices
loving-kindness, judgment, and righteousness in
the earth, for in these things I delight, says the
Lord.

—JEREMIAH 9:23–24, AMP

YOU HAVE JUST read the Word of the Lord. I encourage you to read
the above passage seven times before you continue to read this
closing chapter. Seven is the number of perfection, and I believe
that once you receive in your mind and in your spirit the message the
great I AM is sending us in this Scripture passage, then the rest of life
will begin to come into focus.

When reading my many sources for the research in this project, I
came across a book by Rebbetzin Jungreis, titled *The Committed Life*.[1]
Rebbetzin is the widow of a rabbi, as well as the daughter, granddaughter, and great-granddaughter of a rabbi. She is also the mother and the
grandmother of a rabbi. These credentials, and the love she has for the
Lord, have qualified her to establish a *Torah Center*, where people of all

ages come to hear her teach the inspired Word of God, which is known to the Jews as the *Torah*.

She tells of many counseling sessions she has had through the years, and one of the phrases that impressed me throughout the reading of *The Committed Life* is her advice to those she counsels: "You have done it your way; why not do it the Torah way."

I give this same advice to you now. You have tried to make your marriage work, and you have failed. You have tried to make your spouse be the man or woman you desire, and you have failed. Why not do it the Torah way? Why not do it God's way?

> **HE SAYS . . .**
>
> **Remember this: Your marriage can be a *better* marriage, or it can be a *bitter* marriage. The choice is entirely up to you.**

There was once a village that had every type of craftsman and artisan in its midst—tailors, carpenters, shoemakers, silversmiths, and so on. There was only one trade lacking—a watchmaker.

As the years passed, the clocks and watches of the villagers broke down until none showed the correct time, so some of the villagers stopped winding the watches all together. "What's the point?" they asked. "They're not accurate anyway."

But a small number of people kept winding their timepieces in the hope that a watchmaker would eventually come to town and set things right. So it was that one day a watchmaker did arrive, and the people lined up to have their clocks repaired. But the watchmaker was able to fix only those that had been kept wound. The others had rusted beyond repair.

Our watches—or our hearts—do not always give us a proper reading. But if we keep winding them, if we keep them going, then eventually when the Watchmaker—God—comes, He will set our hearts right and connect us to Him.[2] It is important to stay linked to His Word and to rely on the gift of faith, for in the final analysis, faith in the God that never fails is the only thing that gives meaning to our lives.

The *Torah*, the Word of God, is greater than all other books in the way that Mount Everest is greater than a grain of sand. The Bible is greater than other books just as Niagara Falls is greater than a dripping faucet. The Bible is greater than other books just as the light from the noonday sun is greater than a single candle. Its contents are not made of mere words on thin sheets of paper; the Bible records the promises of the Great Promise Keeper who created the universe and holds it in the palm of His hand.

In attempting to teach some of the wealth that is within its cover, I have found that every word, every letter, and every punctuation mark has limitless meaning. It has been studied by the great minds of the ages, yet a child can find comfort in its message. It is God's blueprint for our lives. It is imperative that we stay linked to it.

God tells us in His Word to choose. To choose for life and not for death. To choose for the blessing and not for the curse. Today you should make a conscious choice to choose for the life and success of your marriage, and make a proclamation before the Lord and your spouse as you do so.

TAKE THESE NECESSARY STEPS

To choose for the life and success of your marriage, you must take certain steps that will enable you to have the relationship you desire with your spouse as you walk hand in hand on the journey called *life*.

First, you must stay connected to the Creator who fashioned you in His image. The Book of Psalms promises that God is near to all who call on Him, to all who call on Him in truth.

When you call on the name of God, hope enters your speech, your mind, and your heart. Where there is life, *there is hope*. Jesus Christ is the Living Water and the Blessed Hope. Proclaim to the Lord with your mouth: "I make a choice to stay connected to my source of life and blessings. I will stay connected to the Lord whom I serve and to His Word that gives me strength and guidance." Do it the Torah way.

Second, you must repent before God, whom you have offended. Every time you have shown insult, anger, or disdain for your spouse, you have shown it to God. The act of repentance tells the Lord you have recognized your sin, have shown remorse, and are ready to begin anew.

Repentance is one of the greatest acts of obedience you will ever commit. You can pray these words: "Today, Father, I repent before You and my spouse, whom I have offended with my thoughts, my speech, and my actions." Do it the Torah way.

Choose to keep the covenant. You must make a decision to stay married to your spouse for the rest of your life. Your spouse may have hurt you, but learn to forgive, for those who forgive will be forgiven. Pray: "Today I choose to keep the covenant I made before God and my spouse."

You must choose to love your spouse second only to Christ, your Savior. In order to be committed to any relationship, you must choose to love. Loving as Christ loves is the greatest accomplishment to which you can attain.

You might have to humble yourself to accomplish this; Jesus humbled Himself before His accusers prior to His death. You may have to suppress your ego; Jesus said *no* to self as He knelt before His disciples and washed their feet. Whatever you sacrifice for love, God will restore to you above what you could ever think or imagine. Do it the Torah way.

Choose today to show, without reservation, the love that God has put into your heart for your spouse. The desire you have for romance must be within the confines of the holy sacrament of matrimony. Any temptation to take this desire outside of marriage is an evil inclination that will deceive you and demand instant gratification no matter what the cost.

Subdue any desire outside of the covenant of marriage, and make every effort to show love and romance to the person with whom you made covenant. God's Word will keep you in God's constant presence. Pray: "Lord, today I proclaim that I will love my spouse unconditionally—as You have unconditionally loved me." Do it the Torah way.

Know that God has a great plan for your marriage. Together you will serve Him in the path He has chosen for you. He takes the most painful situations in our lives and makes them testimonials to His power. We are given challenges so that we can learn to overcome—not to give in.

> **HE SAYS . . .**
>
> **Are you willing to do whatever God directs you to do to make your marriage better? If you will make that commitment—and never forget it, your marriage can be like heaven on earth.**

God always has a greater plan. As you and your spouse wait on Him to reveal to you His plan, determine to be patient, learn to persevere, and always trust in a God who will never disappoint you. These choices will change your life forever. Pray these words: "Today we choose to live our lives for You, Father, and to hear Your voice, obey Your commandments, and wait on Your blessings."

MATTHEW AND KENDAL'S WEDDING CEREMONY

As I bring my section of the book to a close, there is no better way that I know to close this book than to share with you a portion of the marriage ceremony that my husband officiated for our son Matthew and his wife, Kendal, which took place a little over a year ago.

In these words you will find the essence of everything I have tried to teach you in this book.

The ceremony began with this prayer:

> Heavenly Father, we have come into this house of the Lord to unite this man and woman together in holy matrimony, after the covenants of our God, as we have done for all generations past in our family. Today we come to the house of the Lord to honor the Word of God and to continue the blessing that God has given us to carry the gospel of Jesus Christ to the ends of the earth.
>
> May the Holy Spirit fill this room, and may the anointing of God rest upon this ceremony, while we speak into existence the eternal covenant written by the hands of angels in the chronicles of heaven, with pens of iron and points of diamonds, which shall be remembered for the ceaseless ages of time and eternity.
>
> Bless these covenants that they may hold the prosperity and blessing that God gives to those who take them, for God does nothing without the sacredity of covenant. In Jesus' name we pray and ask it. Amen.

Then my husband continued by addressing Matthew and Kendal.

> We have come into the house of the Lord to stand before the Lord Himself, your family, and your friends to express your desire to live together from this day forward as man and wife. You are coming tonight to speak into existence a divine covenant that God has recorded clearly in His Word.
>
> God is the author of marriage. In the genesis of time, God created a man and said it was not good that he should be alone. So God created for that man the perfect partner and brought Eve across the grassy slopes of heaven and presented her to Adam. And because of this divine appointment, we have always felt that

a man and a woman in the house of God also come together by divine appointment.

This is a marriage that your mother and I have prayed for since the day you were born, as we have prayed for all of our children, that God would bring them to that special person with whom they would walk down the road of life with the anointing of God on their lives, because theirs was a marriage made in heaven, declared on earth, and lived in grace.

Marriage is a covenant, which means it is the death of two wills and the birth of one. For the last time in your lives, you have walked into a building as individuals. From this night forward, God sees both of you, or He sees neither of you. From this moment forward, you become a unified whole. For Christ Himself has said, "These two, saith God, shall become one flesh."

The role of the husband is that of a prophet, a priest, and a provider. Matthew, God holds you responsible for this home. He holds you responsible for the spiritual development of your children. And I know that you will train your children in the way of the Lord.

Kendal, as his wife, you are saying tonight in the expression of this covenant that you submit yourself to the leadership of Matthew; that you are going to be the queen of this house, submitted to your husband as Christ is submitted to God the Father.

At this point in the ceremony, my husband began to explain the significance of the Jewish *Chuppah*, the marriage canopy under which Matthew and Kendal had chosen to be married. Three of our five children, including Matthew, have married under the *Chuppah*, or the Jewish marriage canopy. This canopy is a multifaceted symbol: a home, a garment, a spiritual covering. The Chuppah is usually a piece of cloth held by four poles. It is open on four sides to embody the hospitality that the married couple will exhibit in their home. Visitors will be welcomed as they enter into the home from the north, the south, the east, and the west.

The Chuppah is the symbol of a covering over the bride. By being married under the canopy, the groom is indicating that he accepts the bride as his own.

The Chuppah is a sign of God's presence at the wedding and in the home as it is established under the canopy. *Chuppah* means, "that which covers or floats above." At the weddings of our three children who were married under the Chuppah, my husband placed his *tallit,* or prayer shawl, which symbolizes the name of God, on the top of the marriage canopy. It is said that there is a spiritual presence in the space beneath the tallit because the divine Name floats above it.

Four honored guests hold the poles of the canopy, which symbolize the prayer support the marriage will receive. Those in attendance pledge to pray for the bride and groom as they begin their new lives together under the covering of God.

> You are being married tonight beneath a Chuppah. In ancient Israel, marriages were performed under a prayer shawl held on poles by four men. This custom is rich with spiritual significance. It means, first of all, that it is a marriage bound in the name of God.
>
> From the names of God come the five blessings that are in the Scripture: *Jehovah Rophi*, our Healer; *Jehovah Shalom*, the God of peace; *Jehovah Jireh,* the God who is our provider; *Jehovah Rohi*, the Lord who is our Shepherd and Leader; *Jehovah Shammah*, the God who is there.
>
> As you stand under the Chuppah, which is emblematic of the Word of God and the covering of God, so shall all of these blessings fall upon you and your children and your children's children.
>
> Marriage beneath the Chuppah is marriage beneath the Word of God and His leadership, as evidenced by the 613 knots, representing the 613 principles of truth found in the Word of God. As the Word of God is eternal, so shall your relationship be eternal. As the Word is endurable, so shall your lives and your marriage be enduring. As the Word is unshakable, so shall this relationship be unshakable.
>
> Your marriage shall go through storms, for Jesus gave in His Word the parable of the master builder who builds a house on firm foundation. He said, "And when the storms came..." He didn't say, "*If* they come..." He said, "*When* they came..." And they will come, but because you are building your relationship on the Lord and His Word, the gates of hell will not prevail against it.
>
> The Word brings generational blessings. Fifteen years ago tonight, my father, and your grandfather, stood on this platform

and dedicated this church. You are here tonight by the providence of God to continue a generational blessing that has been ours for centuries, and that is to proclaim the gospel of Jesus Christ.

The Chuppah is a tabernacle built for two, and it implies a marriage of miracles. When Elijah rolled up his prayer shawl and hit the Jordan River with the mantle, the water parted. And the sons of the prophet, who saw him, said, "God is with him." Because you have honored the Lord as a couple, so will the Lord honor you as a couple from this night forward. You will live beneath a double portion of blessing, which God has given you.

The Chuppah guarantees a marriage protected by prayer. In ancient Israel, the four men who held the prayer shawl by its four poles made covenant to pray for that marriage each and every day. Those who stand with you on this platform tonight give covenant to pray that your marriage will prosper and succeed in God.

Four also speaks of perfection, for heaven is a foursquare city. Your marriage can be a thing of perfection. Never measure it by the people who live across the street or by other people that you know. Measure it by what God says it can be, because your marriage can be as the days of heaven on earth all the days of your life.

The words from my husband to Matthew and Kendal, which follow, are words that bring wisdom that can, and should, be applied to any marriage, *to your marriage*, to strengthen it and make it all that God wants it to be.

You will learn to give to each other the greatest gifts—the gift of love, the gift of peace, the gift of consideration, the gift of affection, and, above all, the gift of forgiveness, because sooner or later one of you will make a mistake. Your capacity to forgive the other will give strength and endurance to this marriage.

From this night forward, as you honor the God of Abraham, Isaac, and Jacob, His blessing shall follow you. His presence shall be with you. His prosperity shall be upon you. His angels will go before you to prepare your way and behind you as your rear guard. No good thing will He withhold from you, because you have made Him the object of your affection.

There are three covenants in the Word of God: the Shoe Covenant, with which Boaz married Ruth; the Salt Covenant, which is a covenant of loyalty; and the Blood Covenant, by which Christ redeemed the church, His bride, on the cross.

The Salt Covenant is a covenant of loyalty. When two people wanted to make an eternal, binding covenant, they would take salt from the individual pouches that were worn on their belts, exchange it with one another, and recite the contents of the covenant while shaking the contents of the pouch.

The only way the covenant could be broken was for each granule of salt from each pouch to be retrieved, which was an impossibility. This has become perennially and eternally an expression of a covenant that is eternal and unbreakable.

Matthew and Kendal, if you will now exchange salt and repeat with me: "Because the grace of God has brought us together, the grace of God will keep us together, now and forever."

The final covenantal prayer of blessing over Matthew and Kendal can be applied to your marriage also:

Now, may the Lord bless you and keep you. May the Lord make His face to shine upon you. May the Lord be gracious unto you, and may the Lord give you peace. May the Lord bless your going out and your coming in. May the Lord anoint you to fulfill the divine destiny that God has given to you. May everything that is brought against you be crushed by the protection that God Himself shall provide. May you be blessed in your health. May you be blessed in your relationships. May your children and your children's children be blessed, because they are the heritage of the righteous. From this day forward, as you submit yourselves to the Christ of the cross, may your lives be filled with joy that is unspeakable and with peace that surpasses all understanding. May your home, as the Word of God says, be as the days of heaven on earth. In Jesus' name we pray and ask it. Amen.

DO IT THE TORAH WAY

As I was writing the last chapter of this book, our son Matthew and his wife, Kendal, announced to our family the coming birth of their first child, a child to be born on the week of my husband's sixty-fifth birthday. The blessings of our gracious God continue to fall on our family. Thank You, Father, for You are good.

As the world publicizes its prenuptial agreements, which are nothing more than a series of termination clauses, our church gives to each couple that marries within its walls a *Katuba*, or marriage contract. This contract embodies the holy sacrament of marriage. The Katuba reads as follows:

> We stand before God in the company of our family and friends as we pledge to each other our mutual love, trust, and respect. We promise to be faithful friends and companions, rejoicing together through life's joys and comforting one another through life's sorrows.
>
> We covenant to be open, honest, loyal, and devoted to one another. Our commitment to God the Father and Jesus Christ, His Son, will be woven into the fabric of our lives by the power of the Holy Spirit.
>
> We will be overtaken by His blessings of peace, health, and prosperity as we diligently obey the voice of the Lord our God and observe all of His commandments.
>
> The laughter of children will grace our home as we raise them according to His Word. As we share life's journey together, we will witness our children's children serving the Lord.
>
> Together we pledge to build a Christian home filled with prayer, love, wisdom, and a dedication to one another as we demonstrate the love of Jesus Christ to one and all.
>
> We enter with solemn joy into this covenant with each other and the God of Abraham, Isaac, and Jacob.

Do it the Torah way.

As you contemplate the contents of this book, may the Lord God of Abraham, Isaac, and Jacob, our Savior Jesus Christ, be your peace. For so great is peace that God's name is *Peace*...so great is His peace that all blessings are to be found within it.

Notes

What Women Want in a Man

1. Randall Cirner, *10 Weeks to a Better Marriage* (Ann Arbor, MI: Servant Publications, 1995).

2. Rebbetzin Esther Jungreis, *The Committed Life* (San Francisco: HarperSanFrancisco, 1999).

3. Scott Farhart, MD, *Intimate and Unashamed* (Lake Mary, FL: Siloam, 2003), 74.

4. These surveys were inspired from the Wilkinson Family Home page, Miscellaneous Humor, "What Women Want in Men" at http://search.atomz.com/search/?sp-a=000312a2-sp00000000&sp-k=Humor&sp-q=what+i+want+in+a+man.

Chapter 1
Want Number Ten: Faithfulness

1. Willard F. Harley Jr., *His Needs, Her Needs: Building an Affair-Proof Marriage* (Grand Rapids, MI: Fleming H. Revell Co., 1986).

2. Ibid.

3. Bob Moeller, *For Better, For Worse, For Keeps* (Sisters, OR: Multnomah, 1994).

4. Adapted from *The Woman's Study Bible*, New International Version, "Sexuality: A Gift From the Creator" (Nashville, TN: Nelson Bibles, 1998), 112.

5. Farhart, *Intimate and Unashamed*.

6. Moeller, *For Better, For Worse, For Keeps*.

7. Ibid.

8. Ibid.

9. Farhart, *Intimate and Unashamed*, chapters 2–4.

10. Moeller, *For Better, For Worse, For Keeps*.

Chapter 2
Want Number Nine: Leadership

1. Margaret Mead, *Male and Female* (New York: HarperCollins Publishers, 2001).

2. Watchman Nee, *Spiritual Authority* (Richmond, VA: Christian Fellowship Publishers, 1972).

3. Cirner, *10 Weeks to a Better Marriage*, 85.
4. Ibid.

CHAPTER 3
WANT NUMBER EIGHT: RESPECT

1. Jungreis, *The Committed Life*, 191.
2. Ibid., 194.
3. Ibid., 217.
4. Cirner, *10 Weeks to a Better Marriage*, 89–90.
5. Bobbie Yagel, *15 Minutes to Build a Stronger Marriage*, quoted in "What Makes Love Last," *Ladies Home Journal*, LHJ.com, http://msnwomen.lhj.com/lhj/story.jhtml?storyid=/templatedata/lhj/story/data/14115.xml&catref=cat1950002.
6. Jungreis, *The Committed Life*, 219.
7. Moeller, *For Better, For Worse, For Keeps*, 85.
8. Ibid.
9. Harley, *His Needs, Her Needs*, 185.

CHAPTER 4
WANT NUMBER SEVEN: FAMILY MAN

1. Jungreis, *The Committed Life*, 320.

CHAPTER 5
WANT NUMBER SIX: PROVIDER

1. Cirner, *10 Weeks to a Better Marriage*, 120.
2. Harley, *His Needs, Her Needs*, 125.
3. Rita Rudner, *Reader's Digest*, September 2004, 111.
4. Harley, *His Needs, Her Needs*, 125–126.
5. Ibid.
6. James Hewett, *Illustrations Unlimited* (Chicago, IL: Tyndale House, 1988), 342.
7. Avery Corman, "The New Parent Trap: Can There Be a Good Divorce," *Reader's Digest*, September 2004, 124.
8. Cirner, *10 Weeks to a Better Marriage*, 120.
9. Hewett, *Illustrations Unlimited*, 324.

CHAPTER 6
WANT NUMBER FIVE: HONESTY

1. Harley, *His Needs, Her Needs*, 91.
2. Hewett, *Illustrations Unlimited*.
3. Ibid.
4. Harley, *His Needs, Her Needs*, 93–94
5. Hewett, *Illustrations Unlimited*.
6. Willard F. Harley Jr., *Love Busters: Overcoming Habits That Destroy Romantic Love* (Grand Rapids, MI: Fleming H. Revell, 1992), 89.
7. Ibid., 90.
8. Ibid., 92.
9. Ibid., 96.
10. Ibid., 97.
11. Ibid.
12. Hewett, *Illustrations Unlimited*, 288.

CHAPTER 8
WANT NUMBER THREE: SENSE OF HUMOR

1. John Hagee, *Being Happy in an Unhappy World* (San Antonio, TX: John Hagee Ministries, 1993).
2. Jungreis, *The Committed Life*, 43–44.
3. Ibid.
4. Read Matthew 5:4 in *The Amplified Bible*.
5. Read Matthew 5:5 in *The Amplified Bible*.
6. Jungreis, *The Committed Life*, 179–180.
7. Read Matthew 5:6 in *The Amplified Bible*.
8. Hewett, *Illustrations Unlimited*, 347.
9. Ibid., 404–405.
10. Ibid., 488.
11. Ibid., 135–136.
12. Norman Vincent Peale Quotes, Brainy Quotes, http://www.brainyquote.com/quotes/authors/n/norman_vincent_peale.html.

CHAPTER 9
WANT NUMBER TWO: ROMANCE

1. Ann Landers, "Is It Love You're Feeling or Just an Infatuation?", Relationships, The Art of Loving, adviceline.com, http://www.artofloving.com/relationships/5loveinfatuation.htm.
2. Hewett, *Illustrations Unlimited*, 327.
3. Roseanne Barr, *Reader's Digest*, September 2004, 108.

CHAPTER 10
WANT NUMBER ONE: GODLY MAN

1. Booker T. Washington, *Up From Slavery* (Laurel, NY: Lightyear Press, 1990).
2. Hewett, *Illustrations Unlimited*, 118.
3. Ibid., 116.

CHAPTER 11
THE TORAH WAY

1. Jungreis, *The Committed Life*.
2. Ibid., 175.

You have just finished *What Every Woman Wants in a Man* by Diana Hagee. The information you read about marriage was presented from a woman's point of view. The principles the author shared will help you build a loving relationship with your mate.

Now you will want to flip this book over and read *What Every Man Wants in a Woman,* written from a man's point of view by Pastor John Hagee. He will share important principles and stories that, when combined with the information from this book by his wife, Diana Hagee, will help you to build an affair-proof marriage that sizzles with joy and excitement every day of your married life.

Strang Communications,

publisher of both **Charisma House** and
Charisma magazine, wants to give you

3 FREE ISSUES

of our **award-winning** magazine.

WWW.CHARISMAMAG.COM

Since its inception in 1975 *Charisma* magazine has helped thousands of Christians stay connected with what God is doing worldwide.

Within its pages you will discover in-depth reports and the latest news from a Christian perspective, biblical health tips, global events in the body of Christ, personality profiles, and so much more. Join the family of *Charisma* readers who enjoy feeding their spirits each month with miracle-filled testimonies and inspiring articles that bring clarity, provoke prayer, and demand answers.

To claim your **3 free issues** of *Charisma*, send your name and address to: Charisma 3 Free Issues Offer, 600 Rinehart Road, Lake Mary, FL 32746. Or you may call **1-800-829-3346** and ask for Offer # **96FREE**. This offer is only valid in the USA.

Charisma
+CHRISTIAN LIFE
www.charismamag.com

5567